Walk With Me

Harry Giglio

Dedication

TO MARY

Preface

The moment I stepped off our plane in Italy, I reached down and placed my hand on the ground. It did not matter to me that it was an asphalt tarmac. I knew that 70 feet below my hand Roman soldiers once walked. I had come full circle. I had arrived home to the land of my ancestors. I was back to the land that made me a couple of generations ago and I delighted in the fact that everyone could pronounce my name. That is the fuel that drives my creative passion in Italy.

The countless glorious structures still whisper the breath of the multitude of souls that once occupied small homes to coliseums. These structures seem to be as much alive as the people who walk their streets and live within their walls. The past and the present are beautifully intertwined.

Every evening in nearly every town, the residents stroll the streets. Some are families, some are groups of kids, some are lovers, and others are just old friends. They interact with one another, enjoy gelato or espresso, some laugh, some just slowly stroll quietly. All are just enjoying the bond of family, friendships and fellow townspeople. It is wonderful to be a part of it.

Italy inspires me to open my mind's eye, to see the beauty of the world and the people around me. Italy has a way of resetting my mind and my outlook on life and makes me realize there is a better way to live, a way that we all could live. There is so much of Italy and its people that I simply have no words for. I hope these images will reveal this beauty, this energy and this magical culture to you.

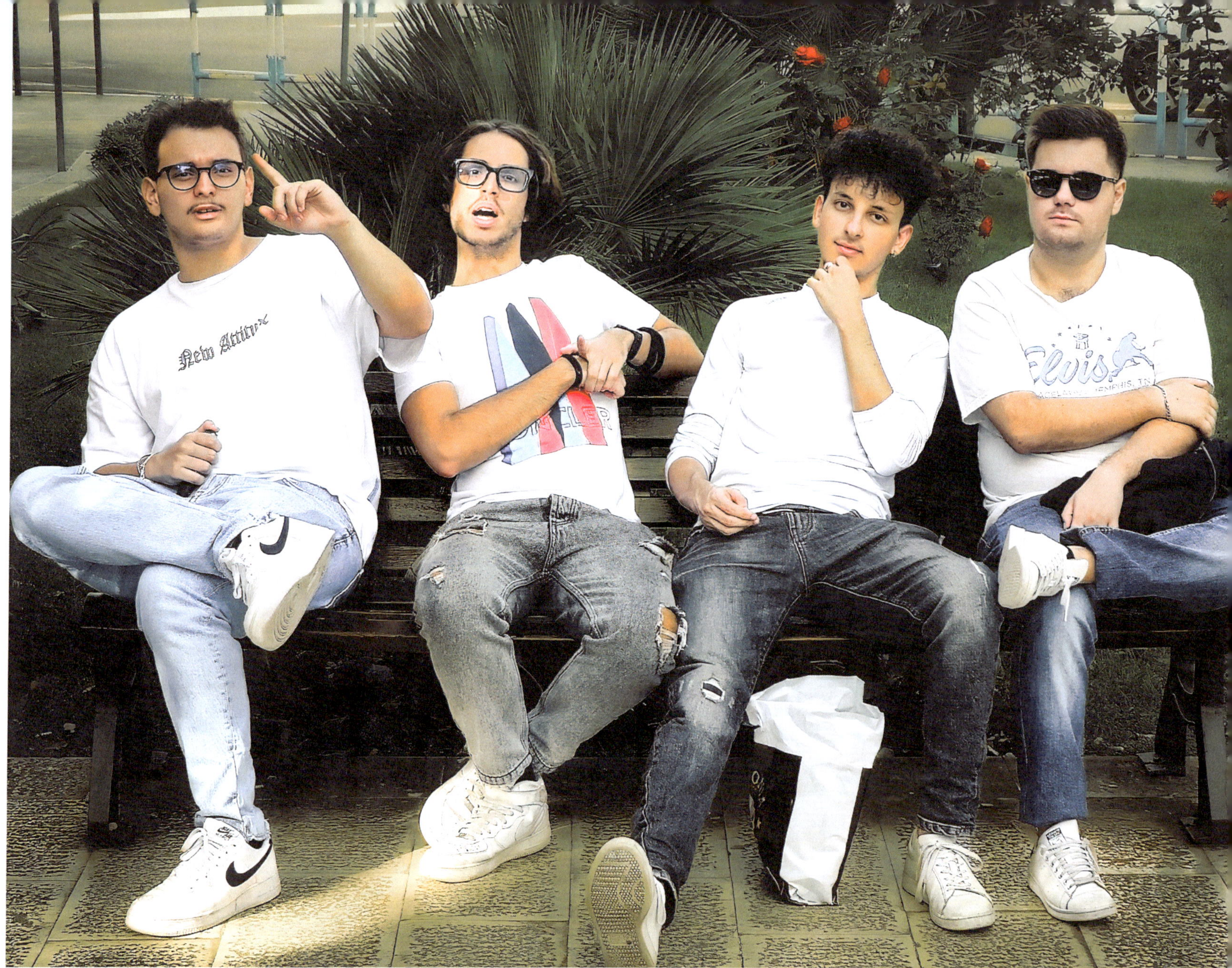

Elvis
Bari:
A group of boys ham it up for my camera and then get up to offer my wife and I their bench.
Respect for elders is a part of the culture..like it should be everywhere.

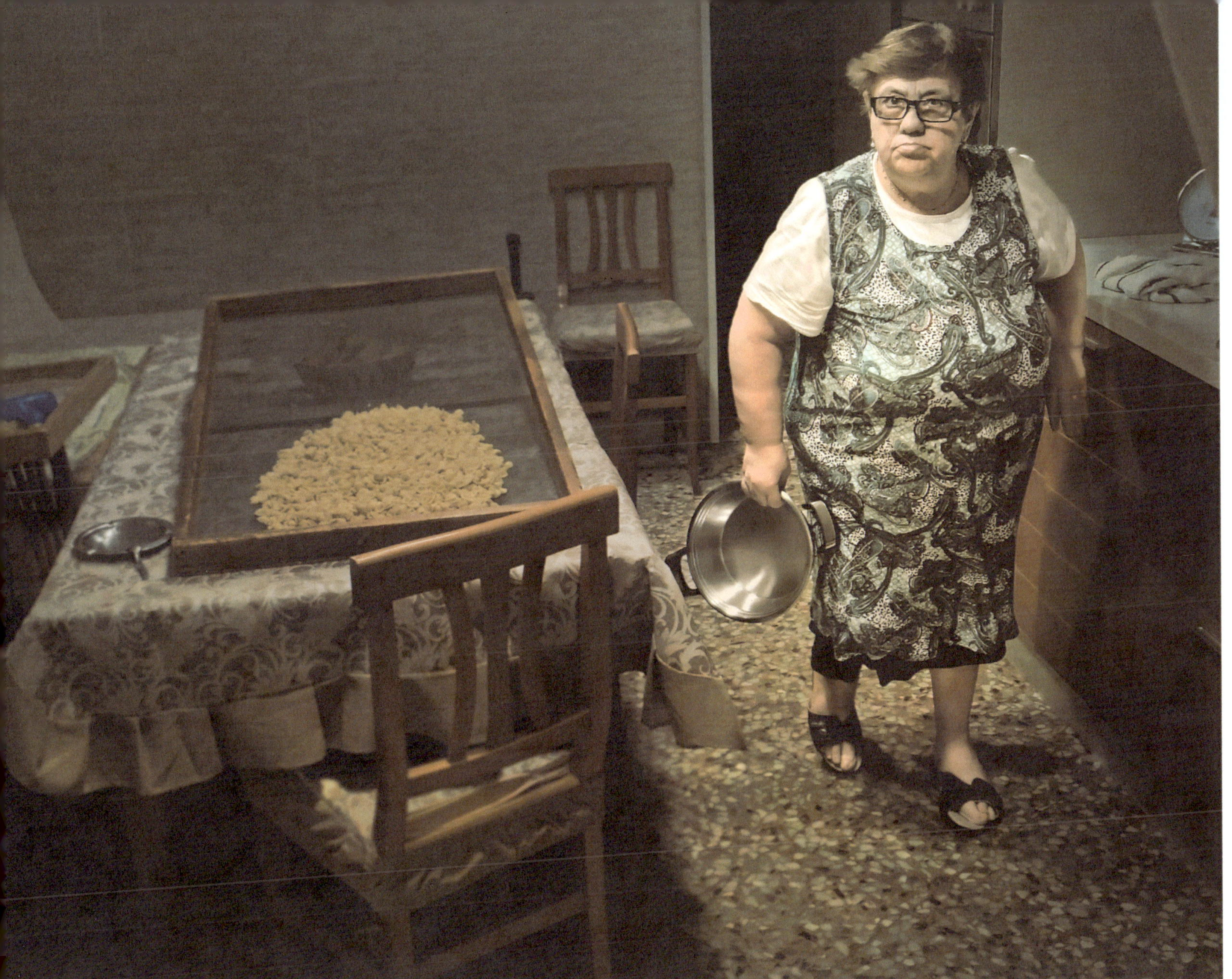

Pasta Nonna
Bari;
A stern look was quickly brought to smiles when I purchased a pound of her handmade pasta.
" Take pictures but buy my pasta"

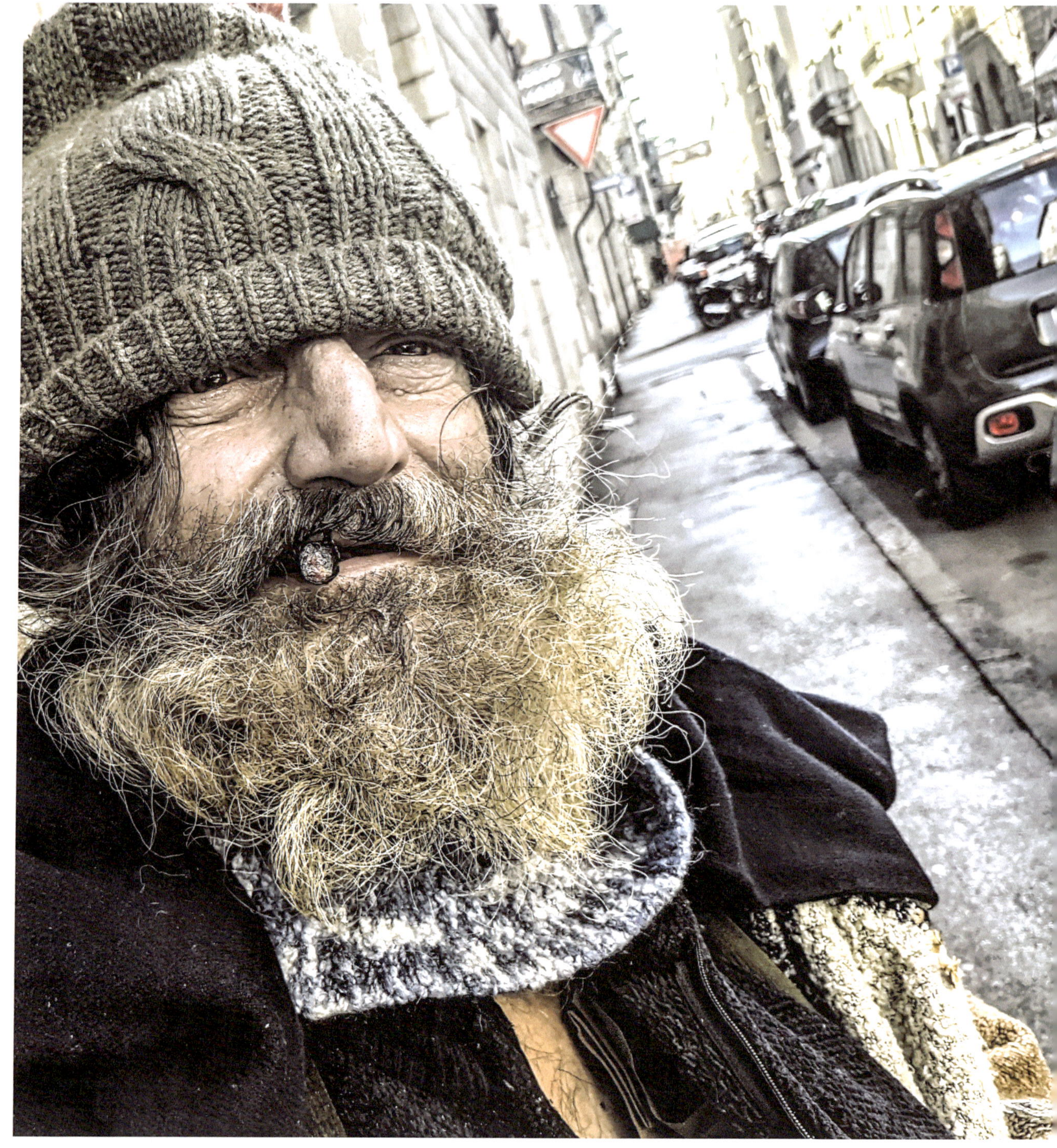

Homeless
Trieste:
Amidst the streets, a haunting face reflects the plight of homelessness in Trieste.

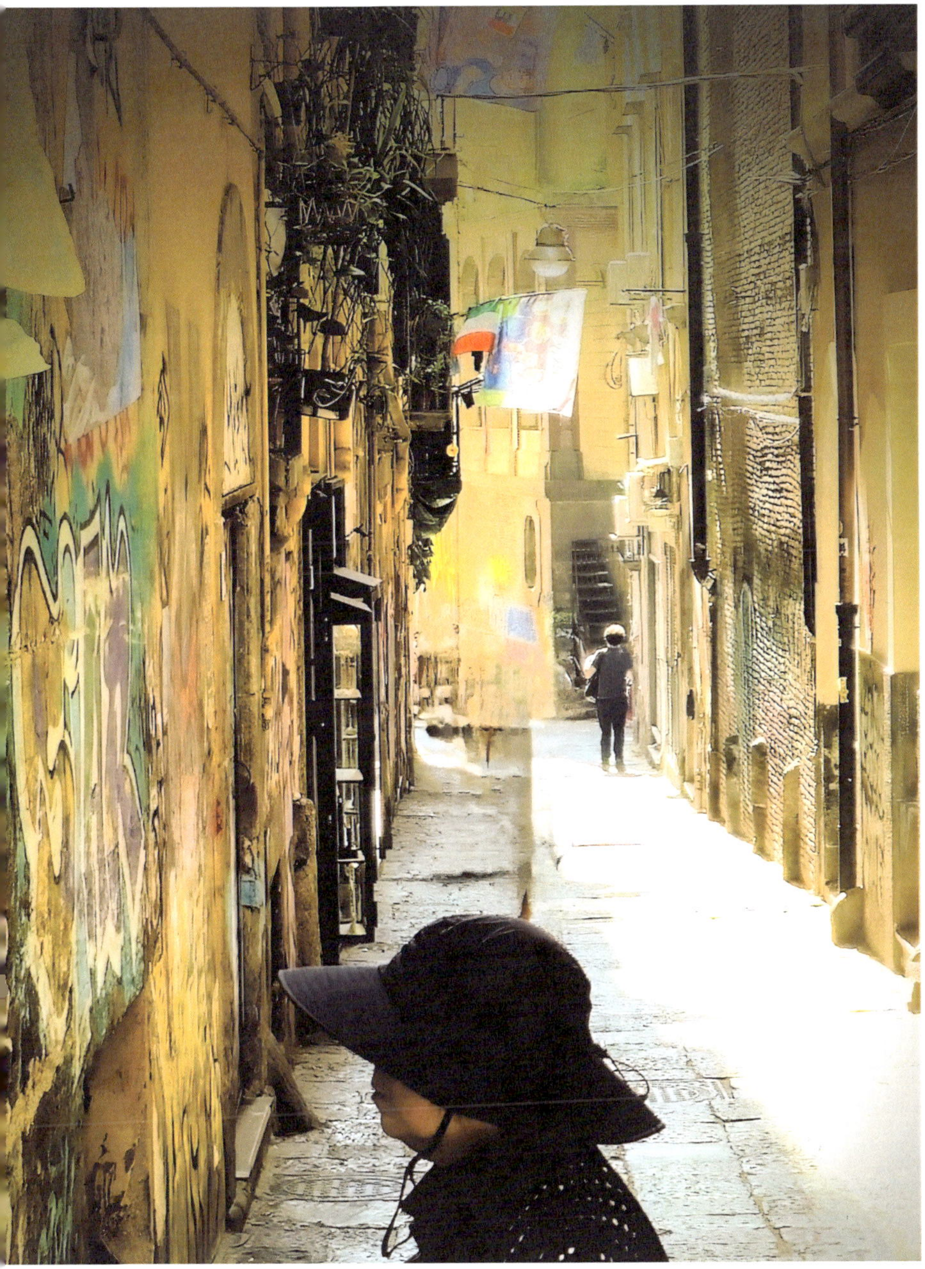

Backstreet Love
Monopoli:
Embracing is common in Italy but this was one scene I didnt linger on very long.

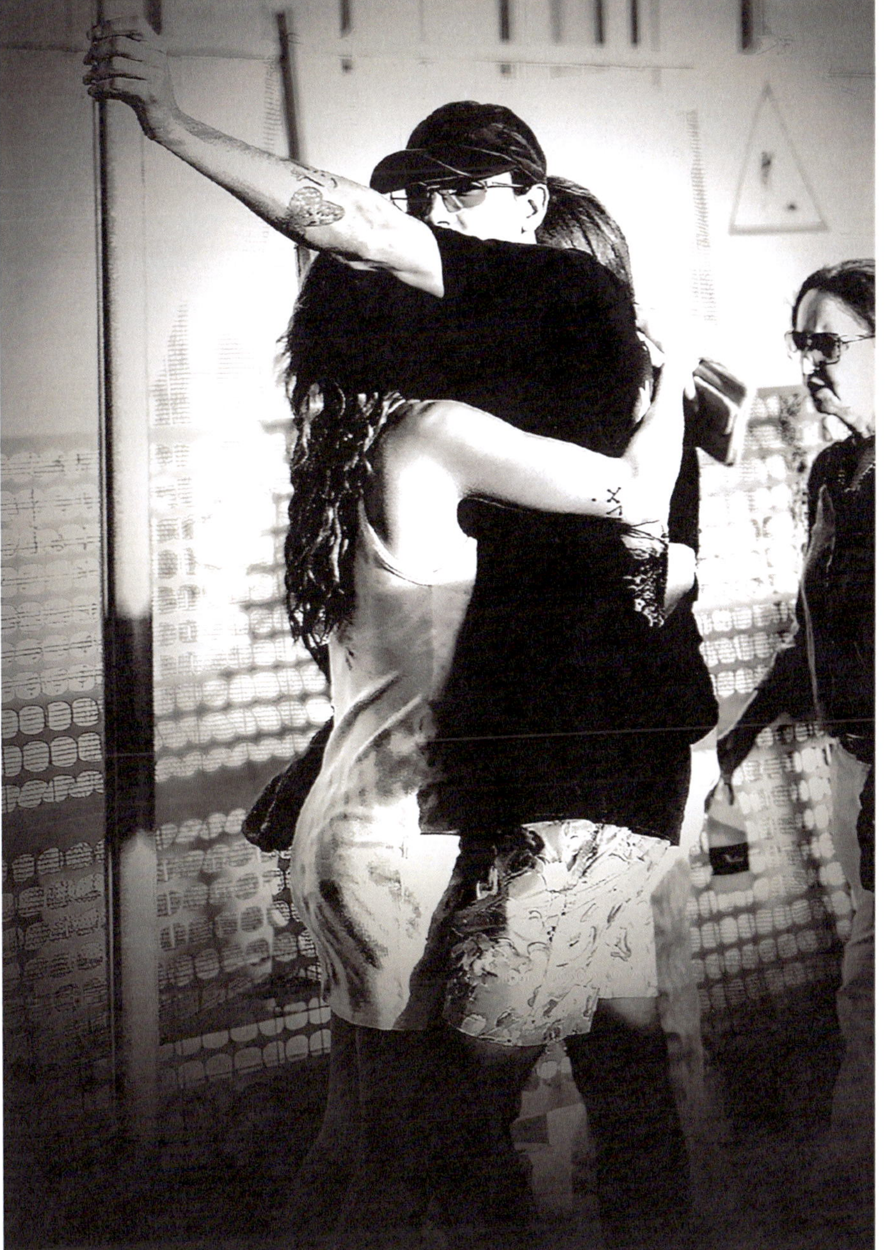

Black Hat
Naples:
A woman, adorned in a black hat and mourning clothes, crosses my path like a cat in a narrow alley.

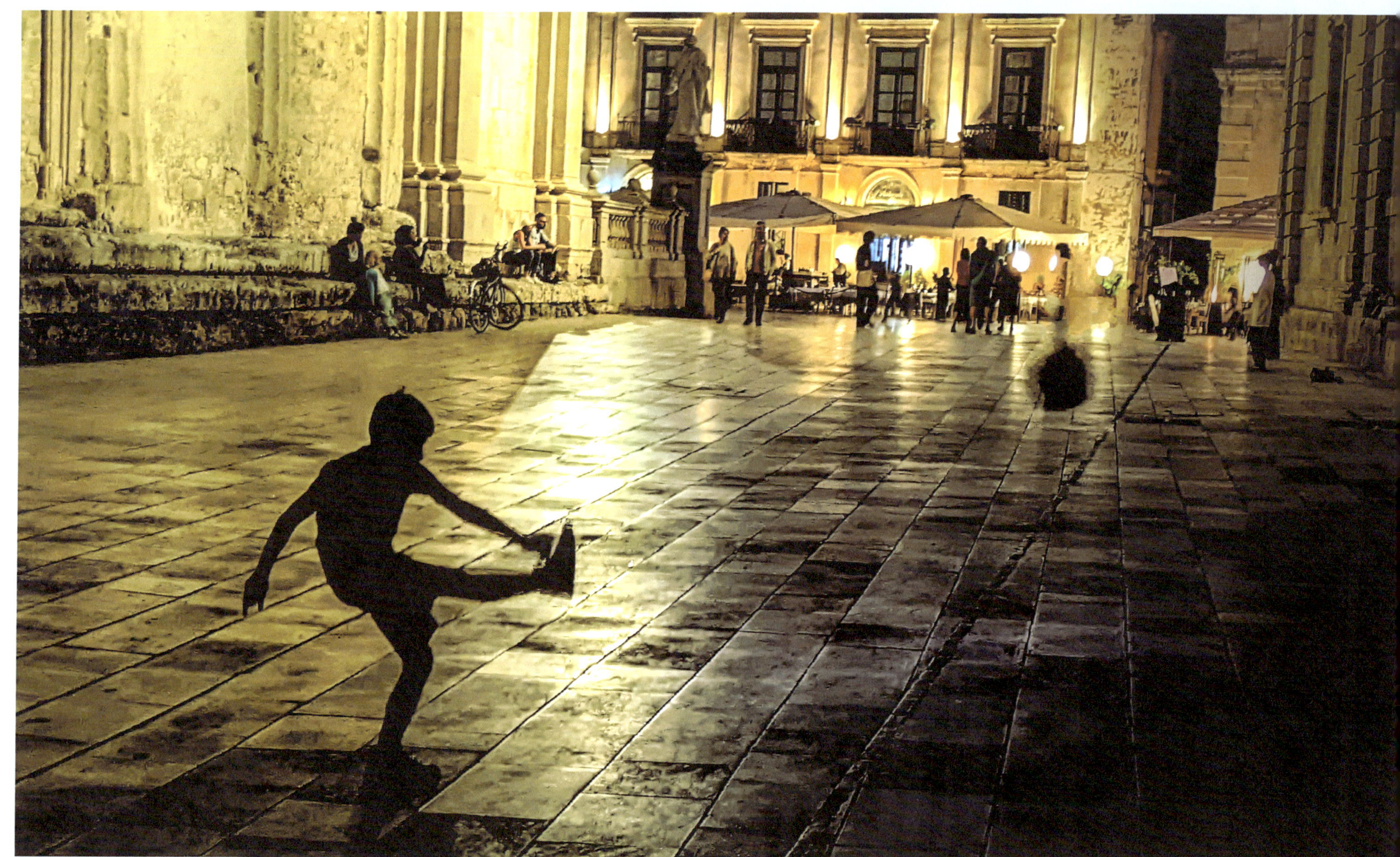

Soccer Homework
Ortigia:
A boy uses an ancient wall to perfect his evening accuracy.

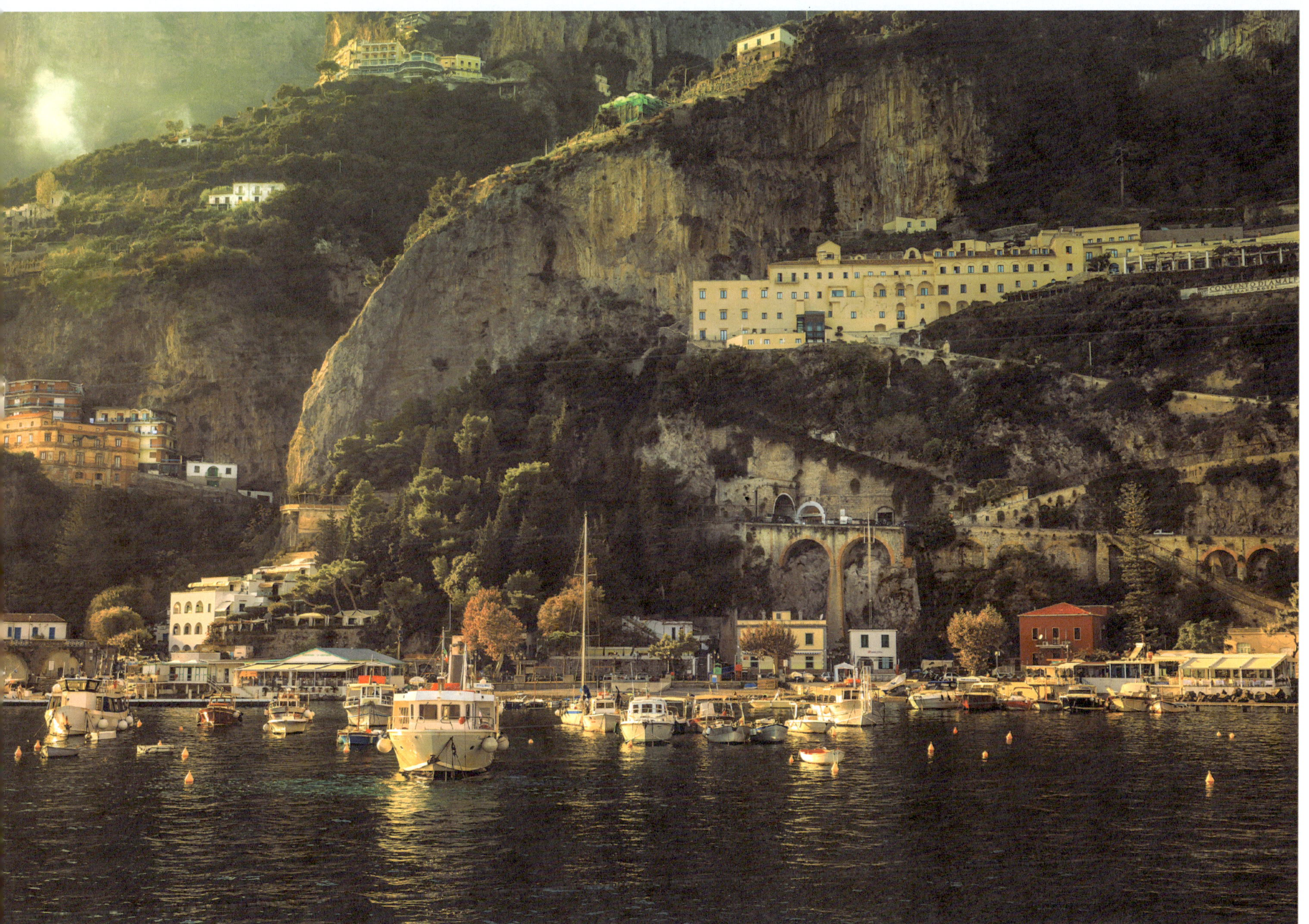

Sundown
Amalfi:
The sun rakes across the curves and lines of the Amalfi coast as if guided by the hand of The Almighty.

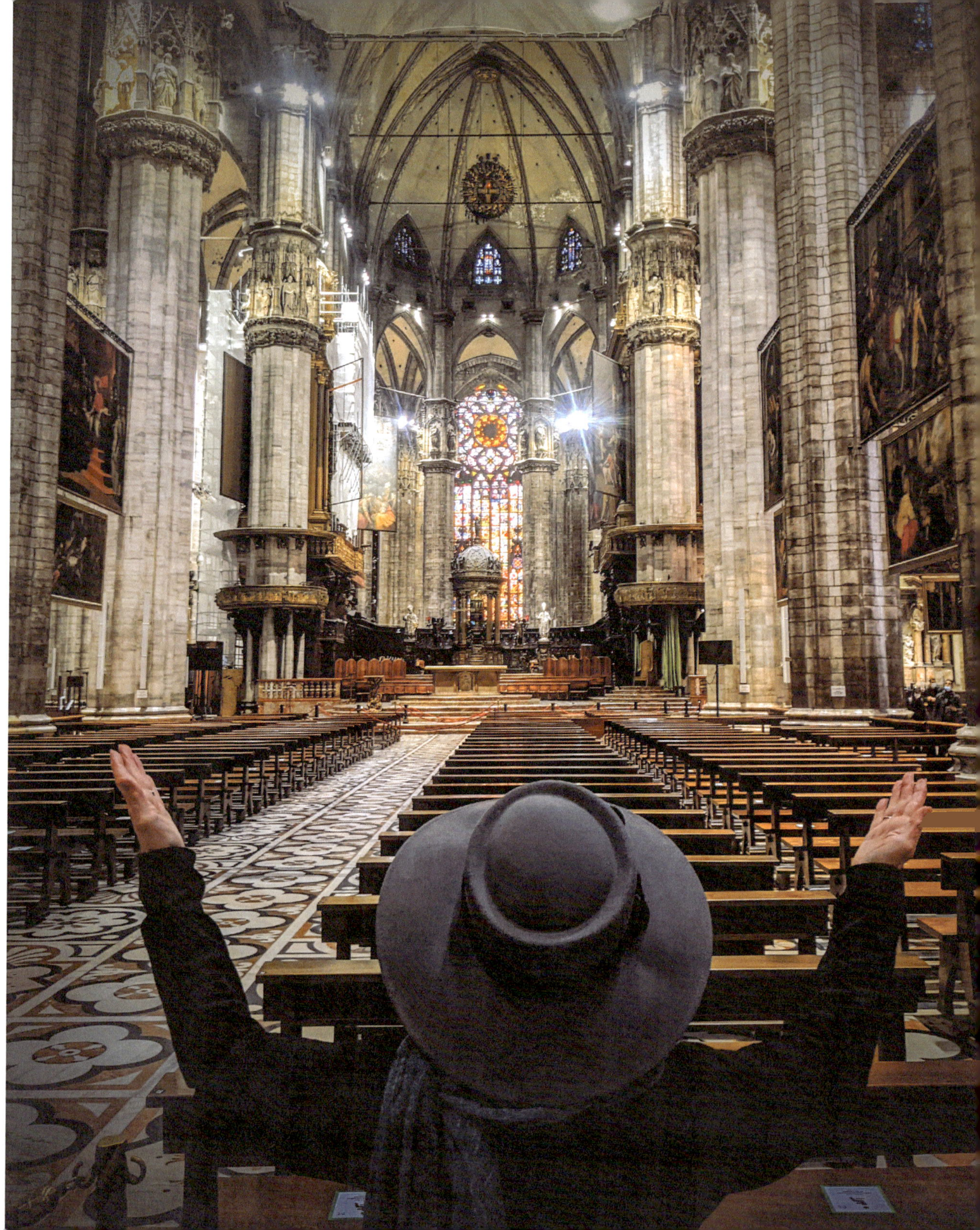

Divine Moments
Milan:
A woman raises her hands in praise in the majestic Duomo di Milano as prayers whisper from her lips.

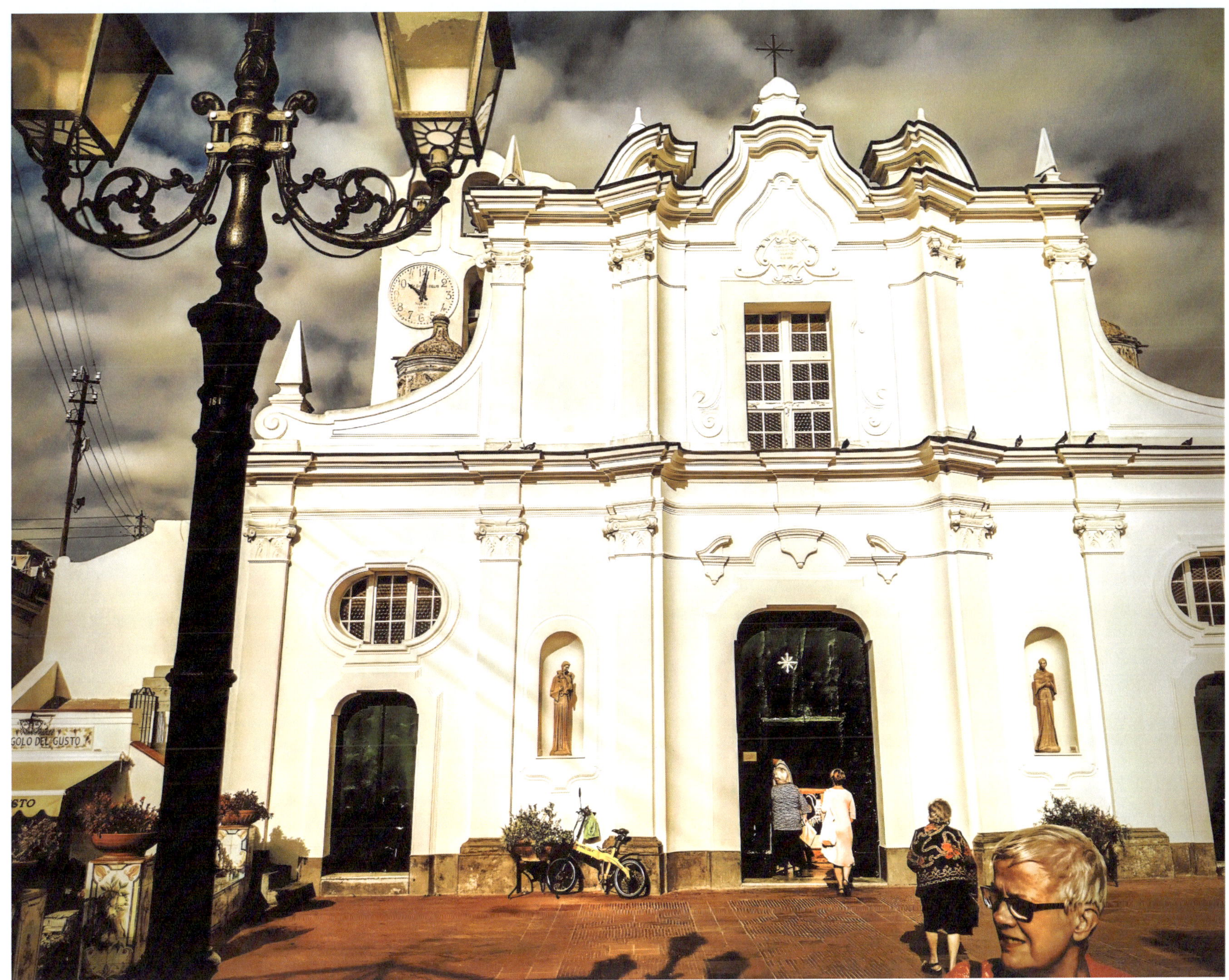

Sunday Mass
Anacapri:
The rural faithful and a few tourists gather to the clanging bells, just as they have every week for hundreds of years.

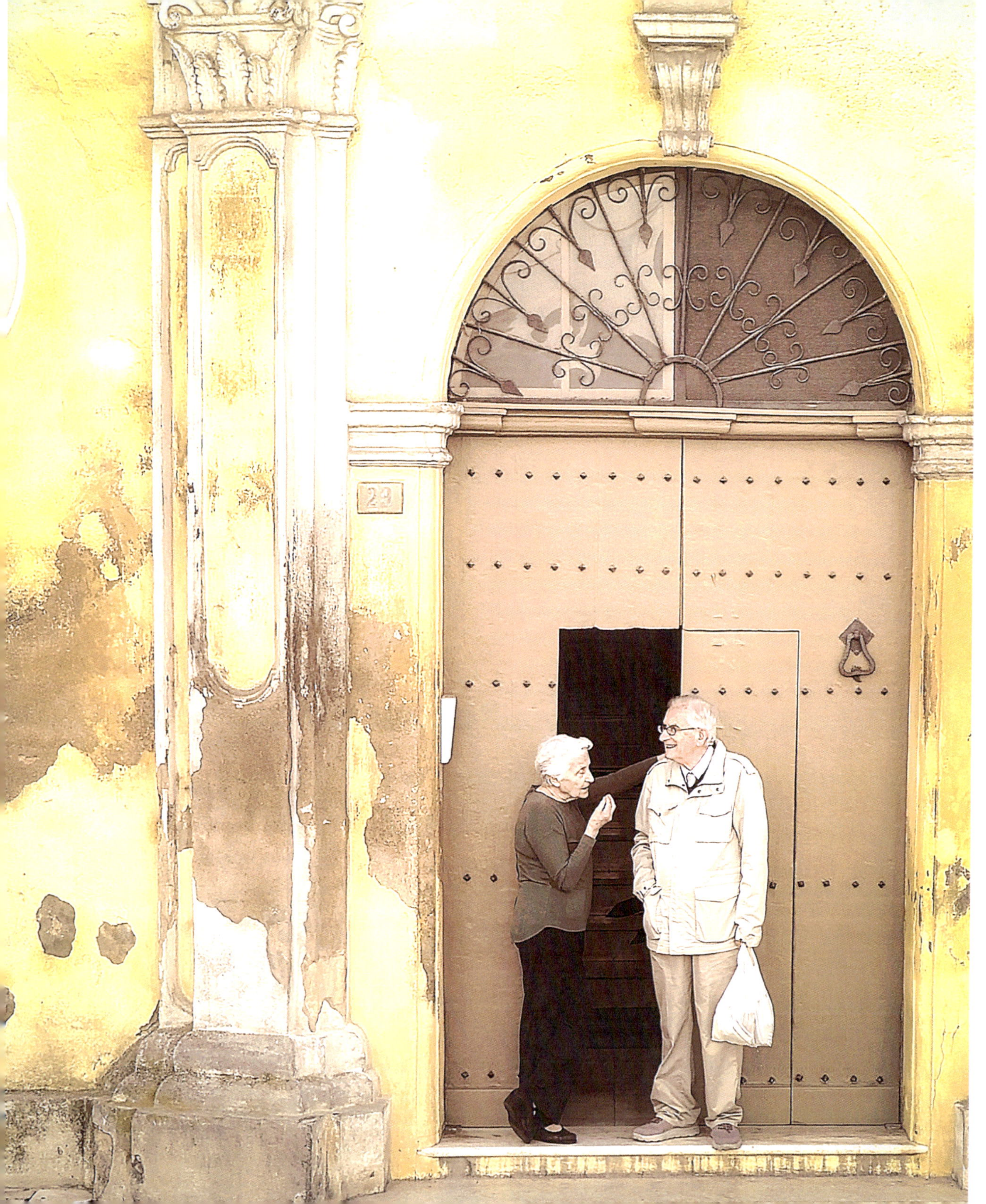

Archway
Matera:
Brother and sister converse outside the rustic cathedral just as they have many times since they were children. You can almost feel the centuries of generations, as if the walls resurrect their memory like a time machine.

Going Home
Bari:
Workers make their way home to their simple flats as the early morning begins and all is closed for the day. Sometimes it is hard to tell if the moving shadows are real or remnants of a soul that doesn't want to leave.

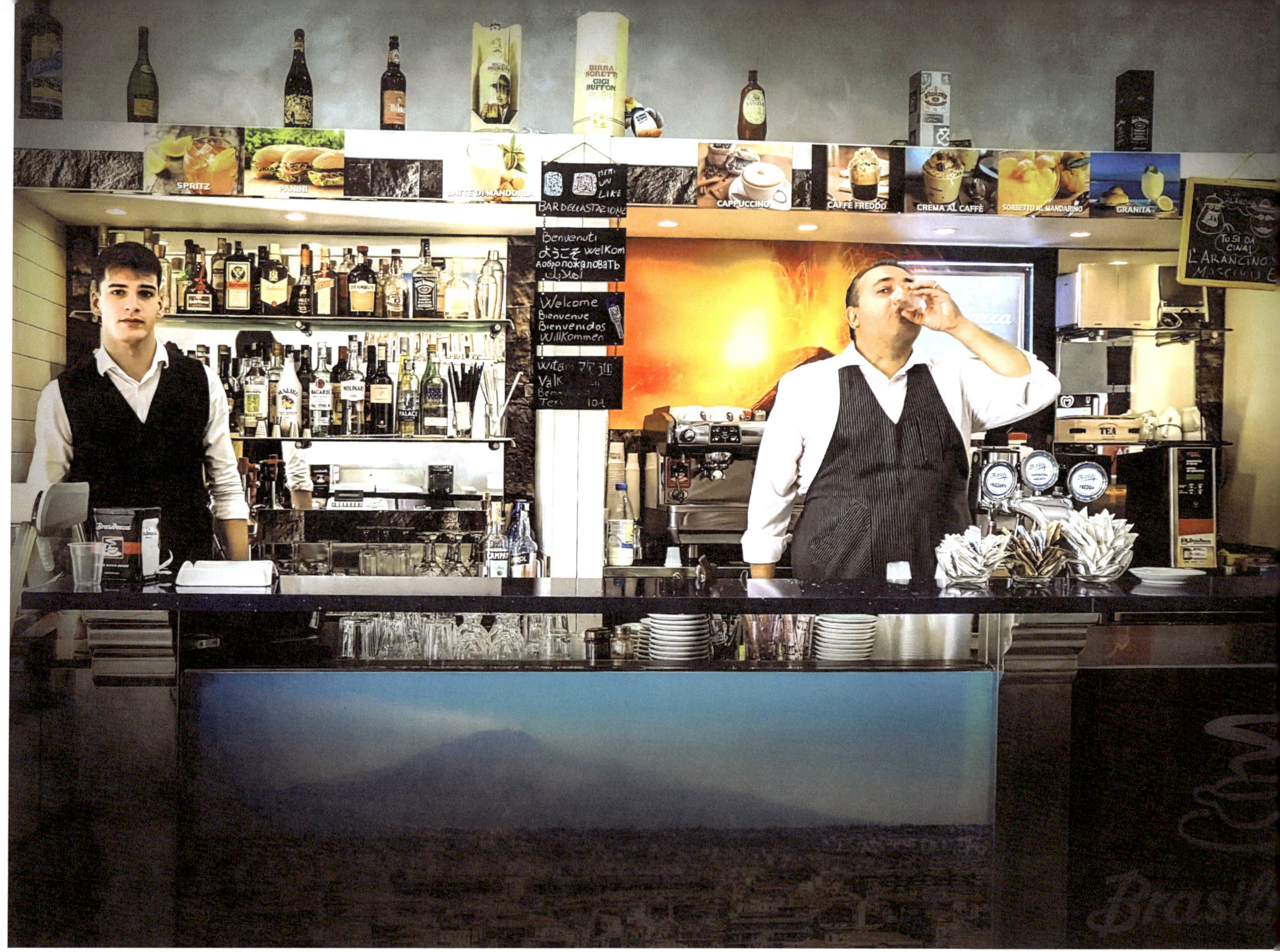

Quick Sho

Catania

The town's best espresso and pastry can be savored right here at this train station. Servers are respected and considered professional workers. Many men work in this field all of their life making a respectable living to support their families. All eager to engage in conversation and share insights into their culture

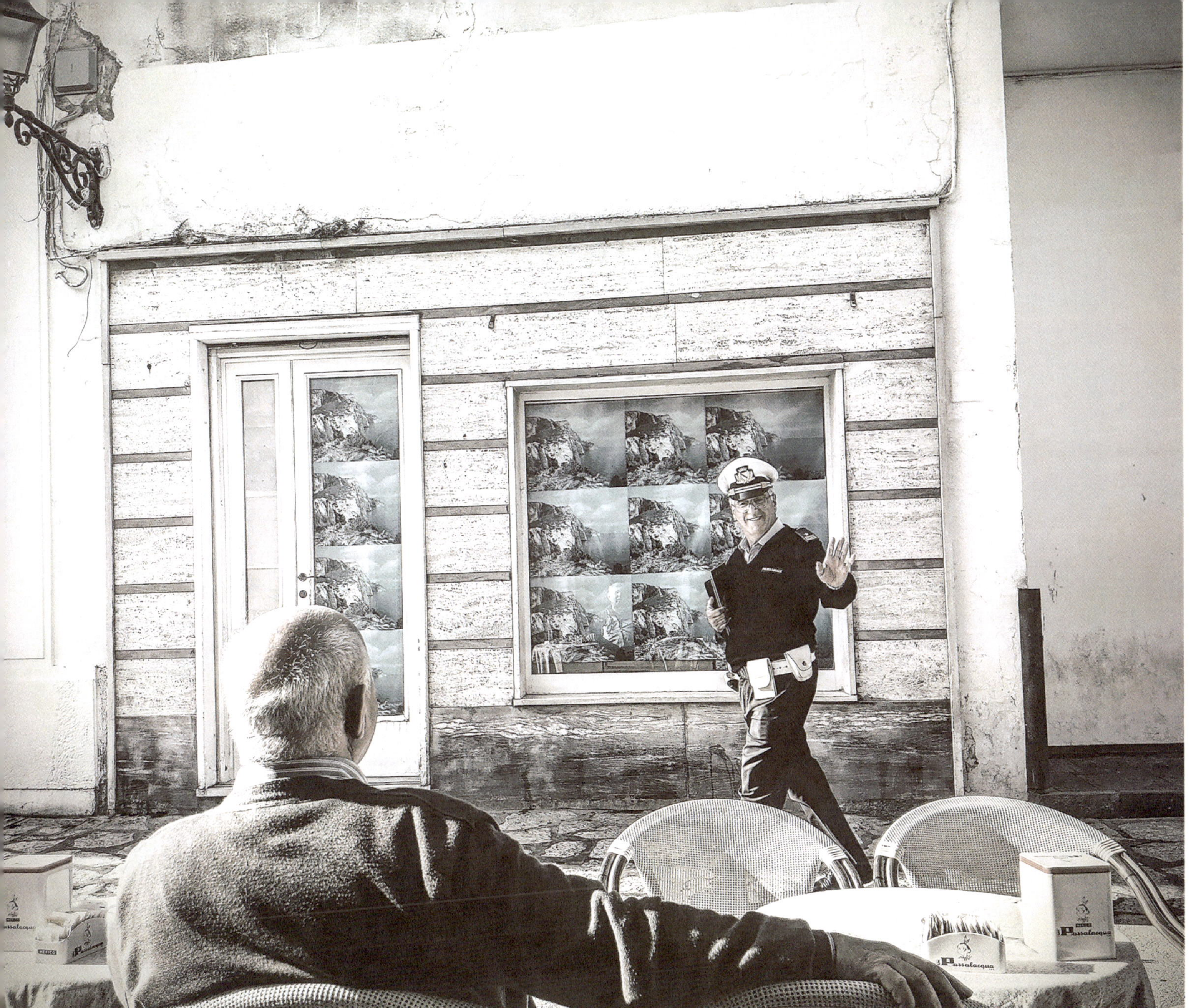

Buongiorno
Anacapri:
A government officer warmly greets a few fiends on his way to the station.

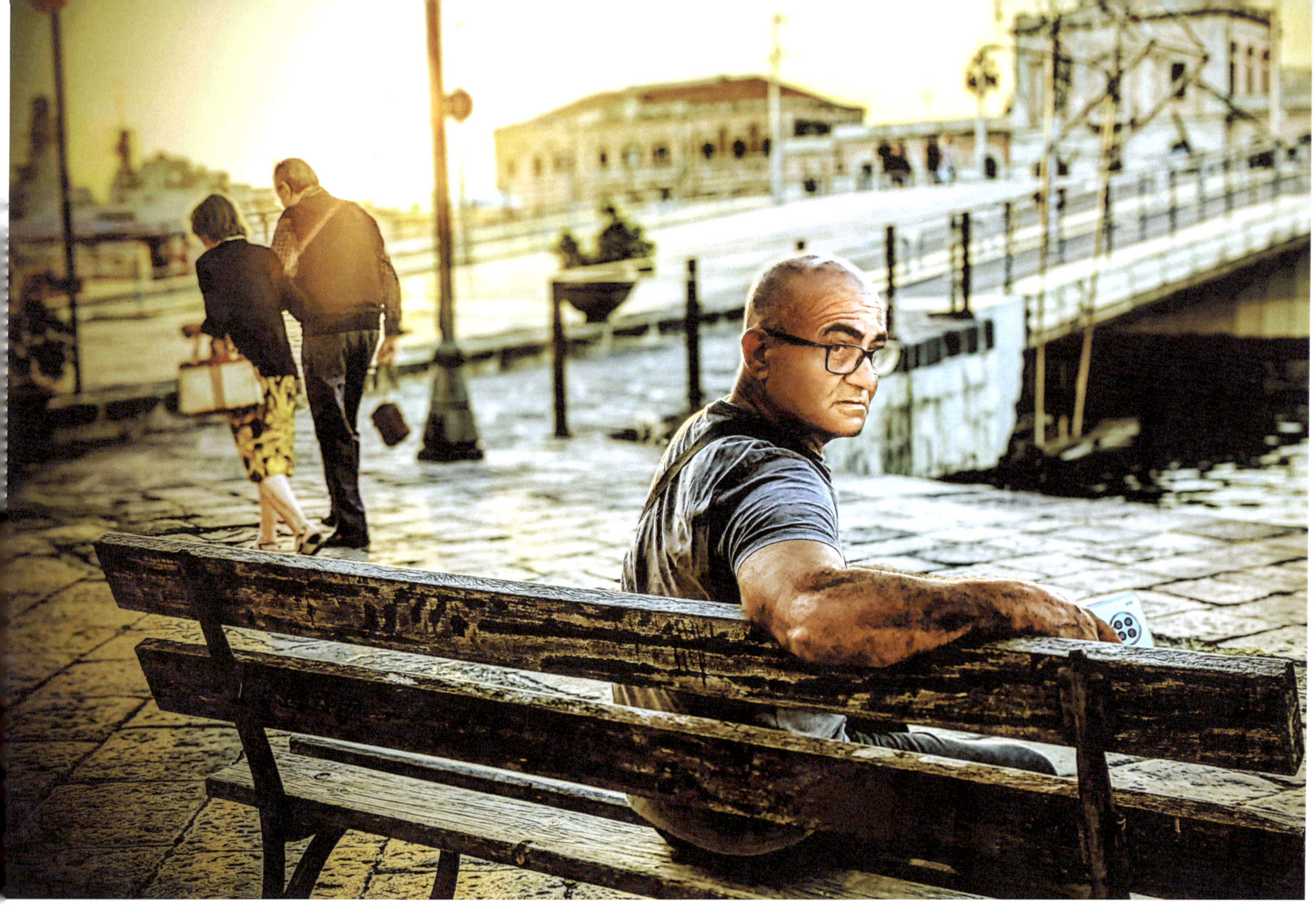

Mechanic
Siracusa:
A vacationing couple and a local worker relax in the warm sunset. For a split second… a perfect composition.

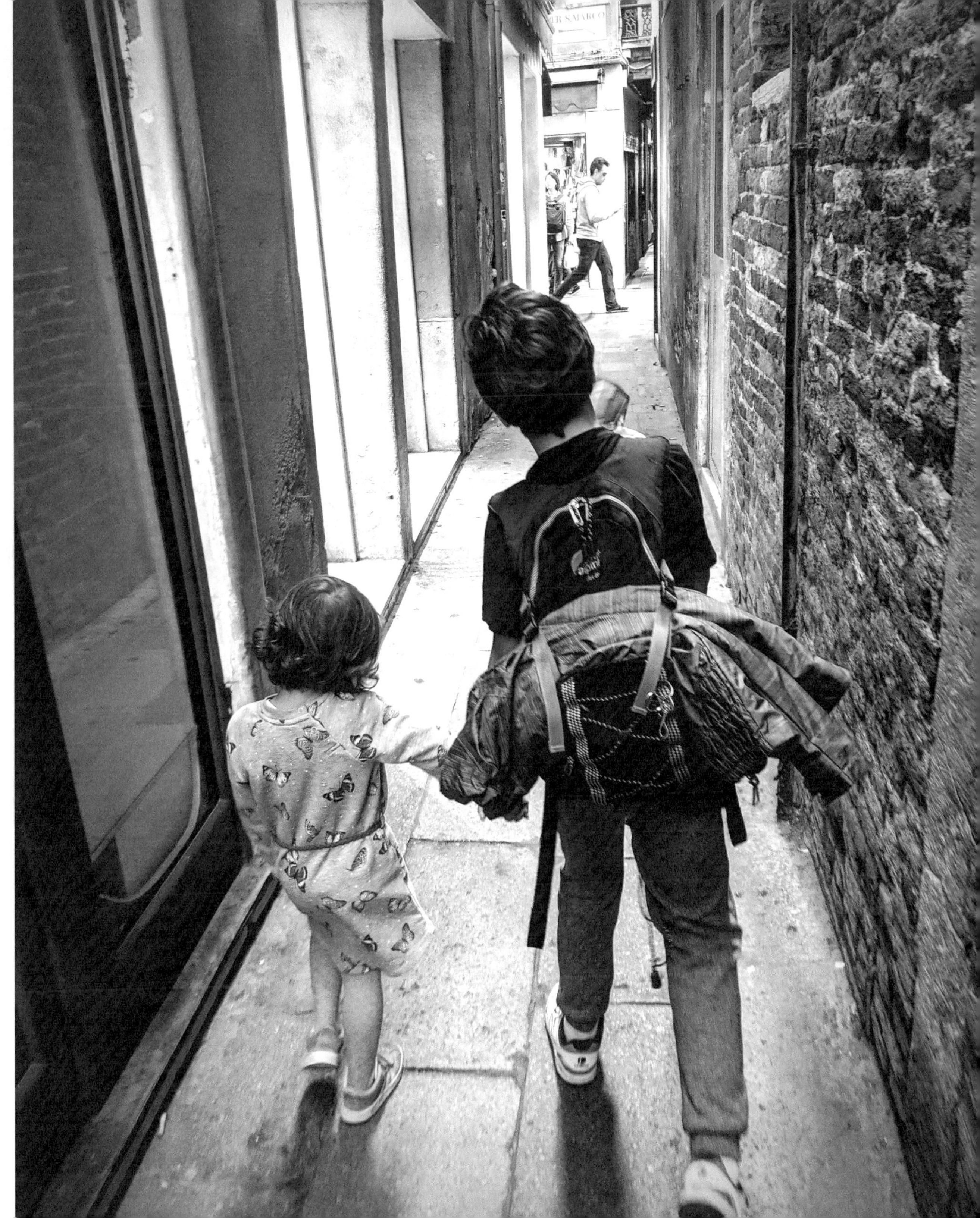

Lost
Venice:
A brother and sister search for their father as he passes just ahead of them while texting.

They reunited seconds later.

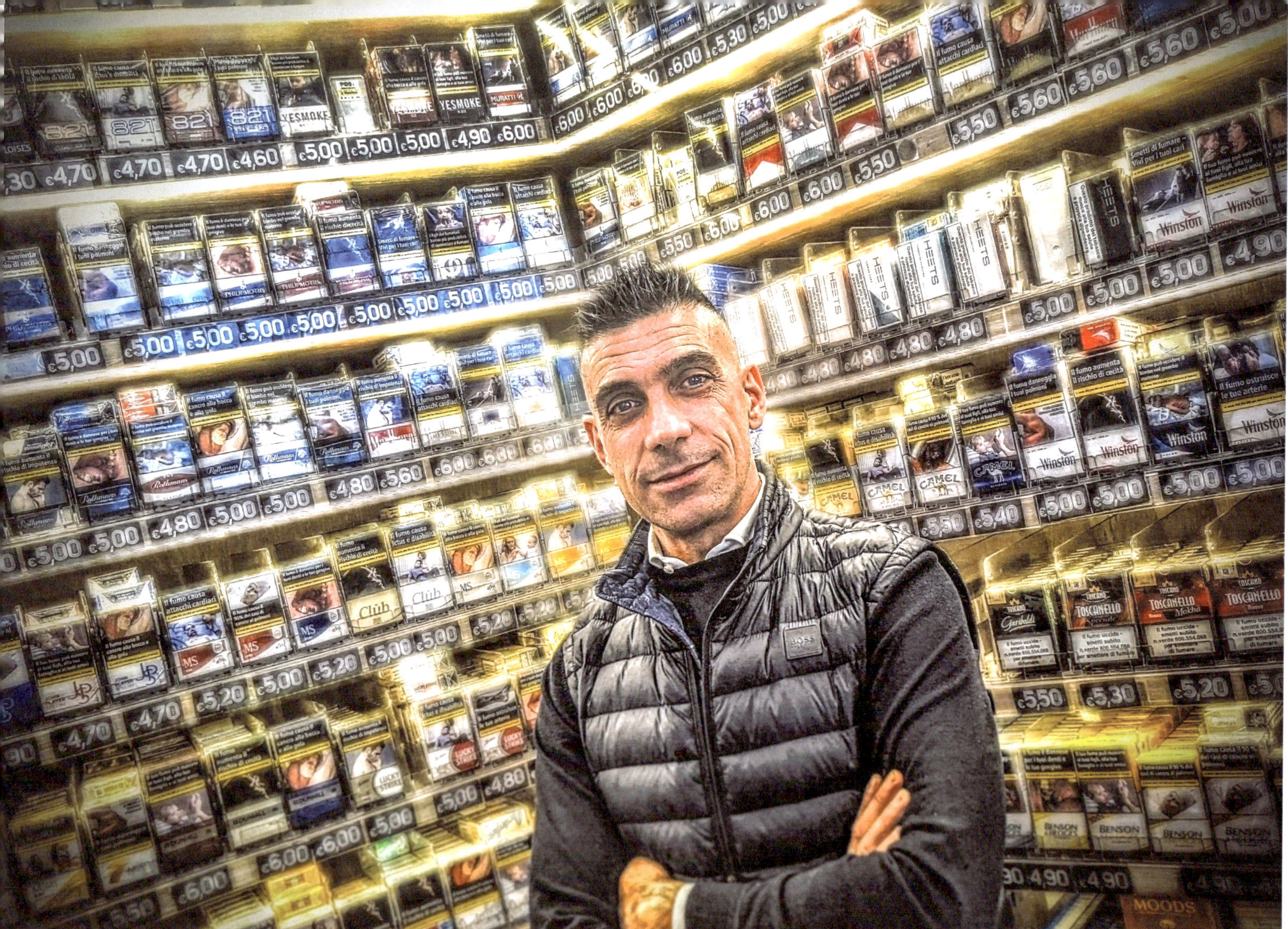

Smokin
Milan:
It seems like everyone smokes in Italy..at this store smokes, caffe and pastries start the day of the multitudes.

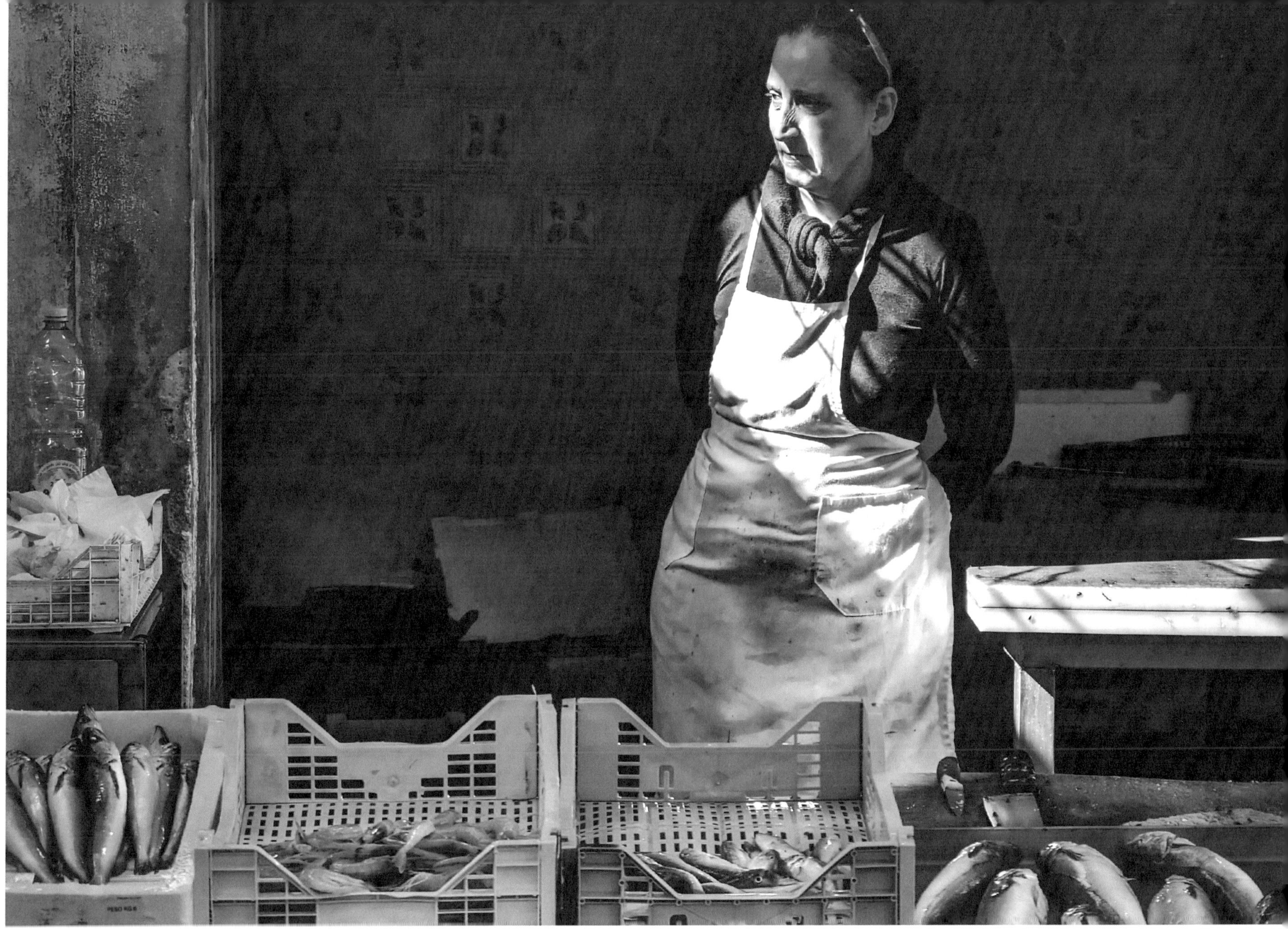

Fish Lady
Ortigia:
Lost in her thoughts as if in a different place, she begins another day as the sunrise warms her face.

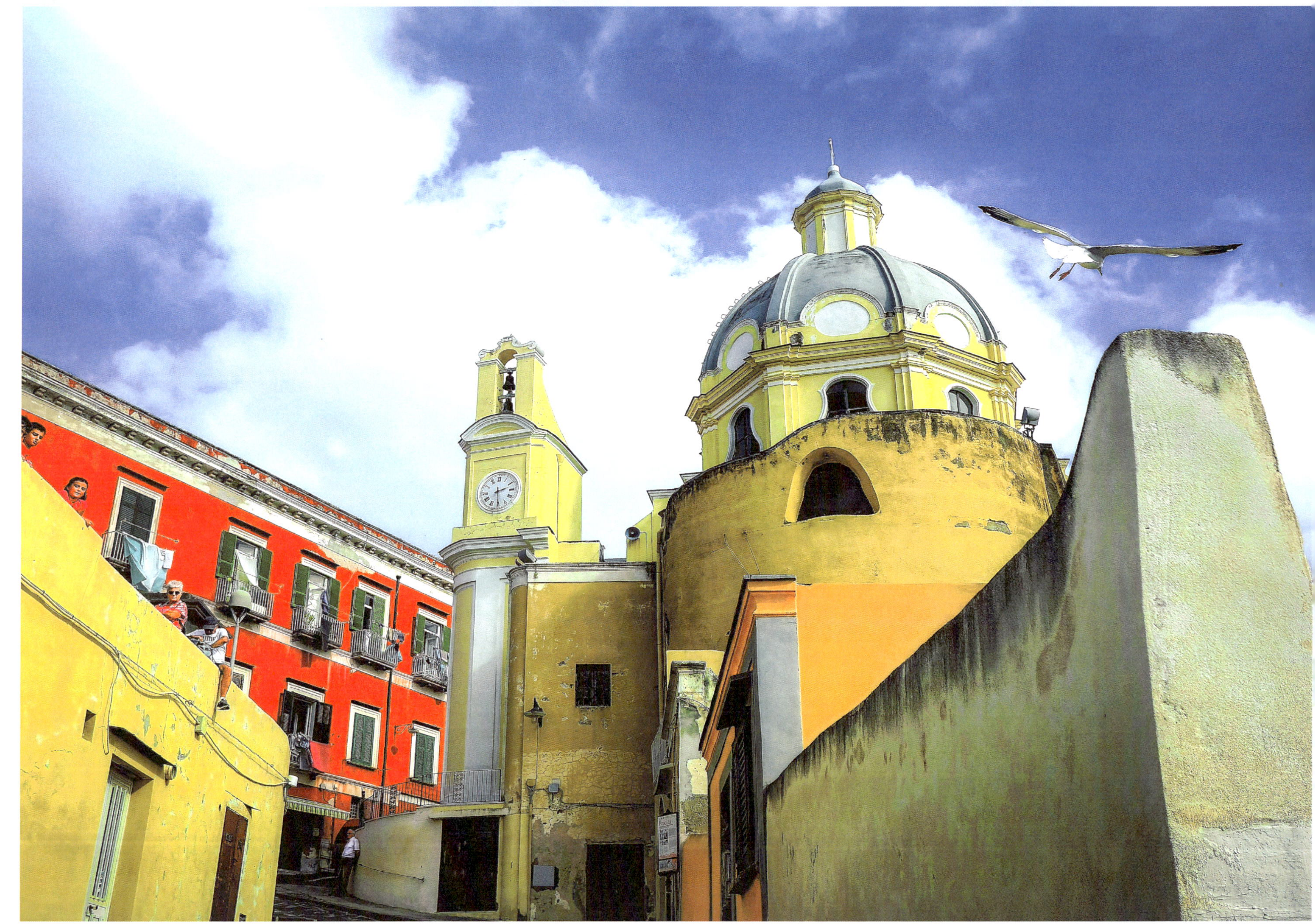

Heavenly Flight
Procida:
The small and colorful Church of Procida. The people appear as toys in this surreal setting while a reminder of the Divine circles overhead.

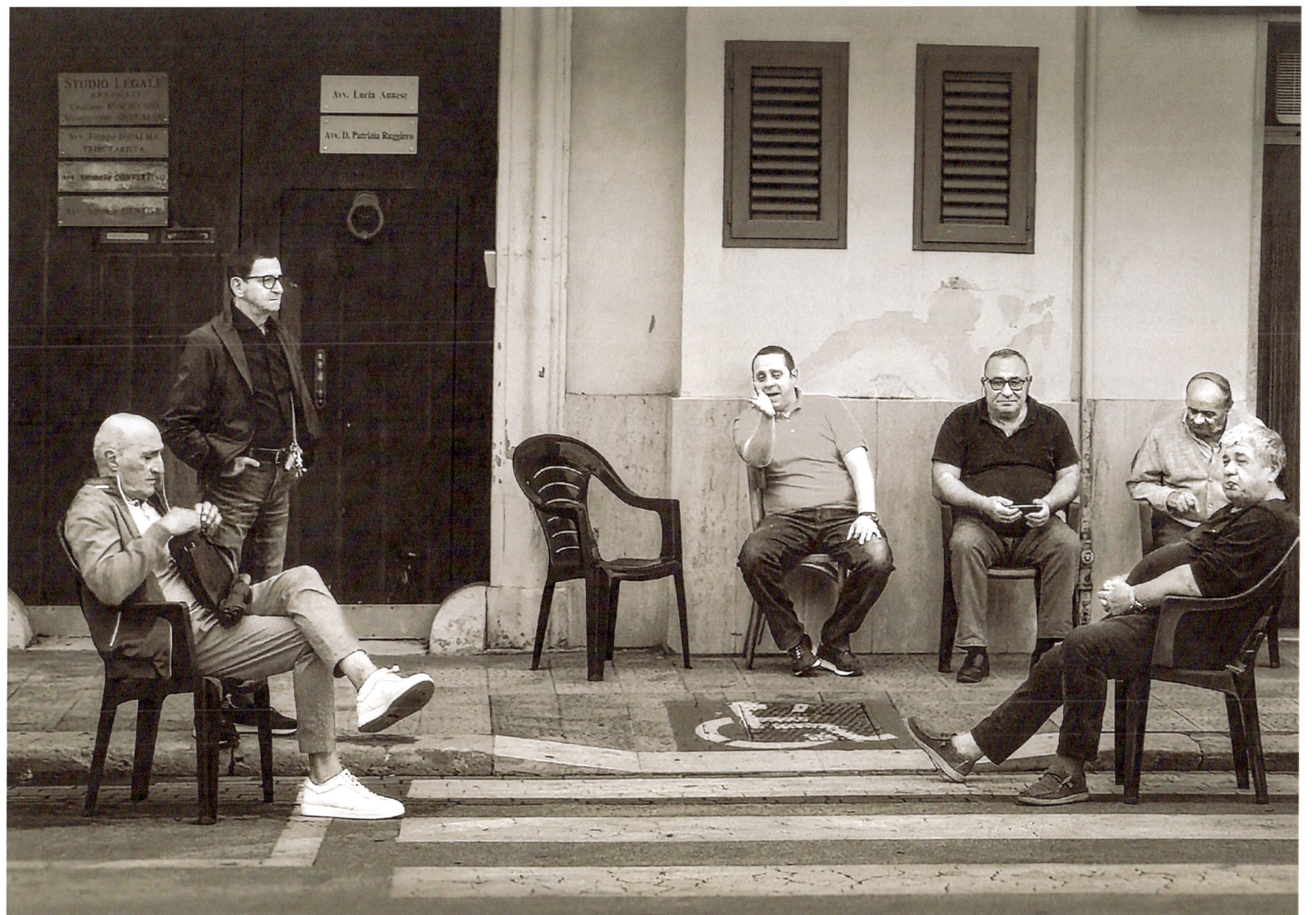

Contempaltion
Monopoli:
A group of seasoned gentlemen, the board of directors, sit together in profound silence.

Joy
Monopoli:
Little girls rejoice on the beach, capturing the carefree spirit of the sea.

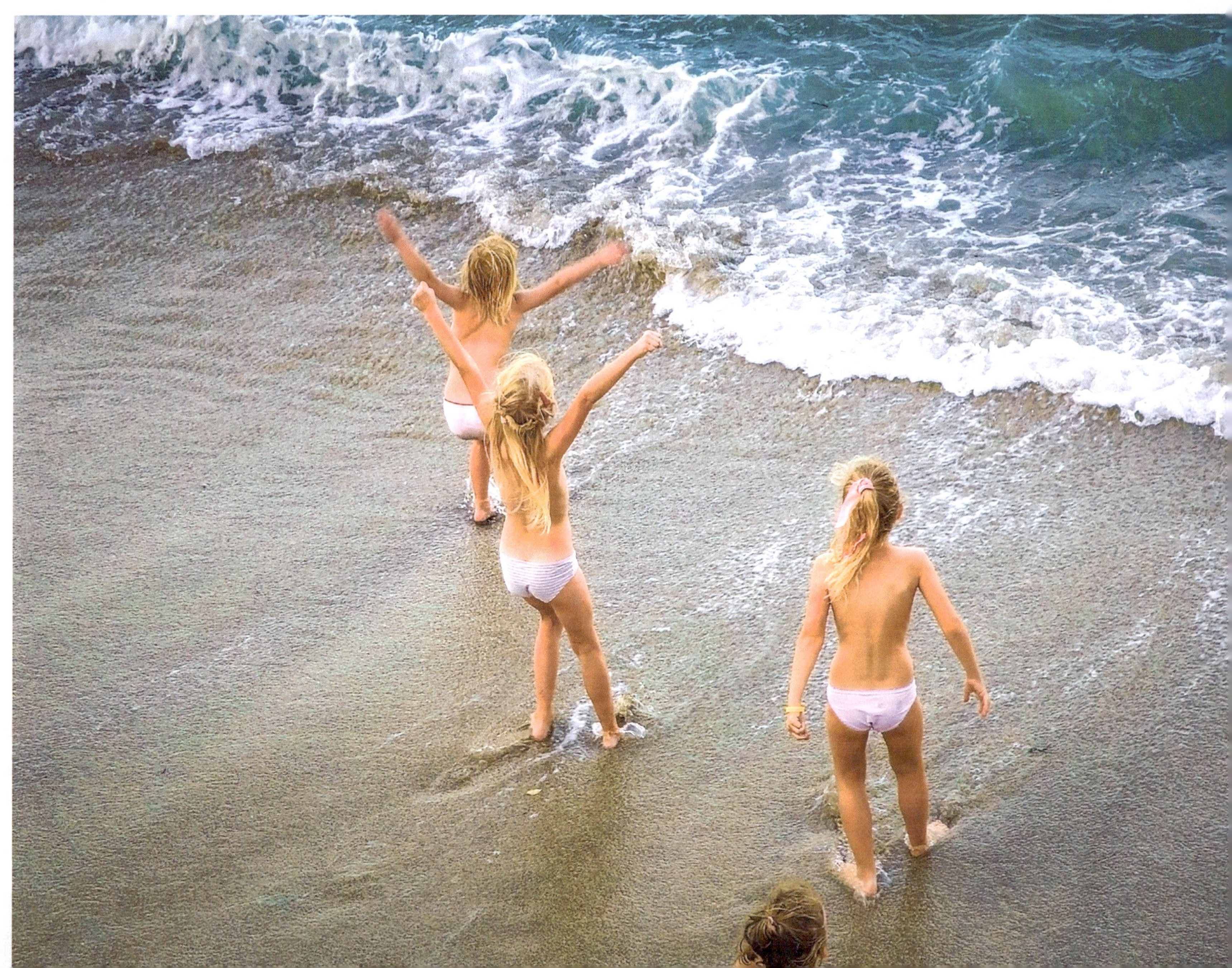

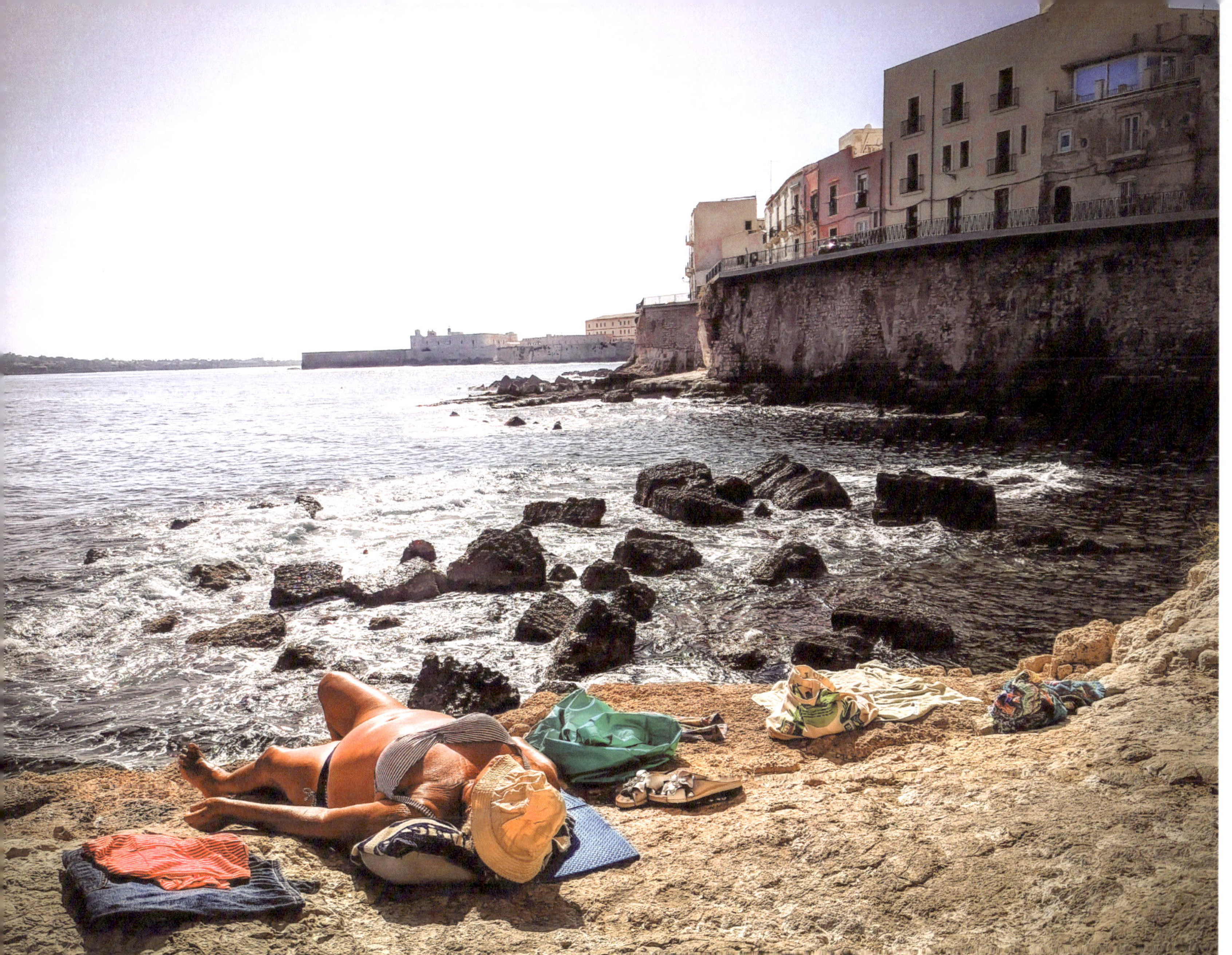

Burn
Ortigia:
A woman, captivated by the mid-day sun, succumbs to sleep, basking in the warmth that envelops Ortigia.

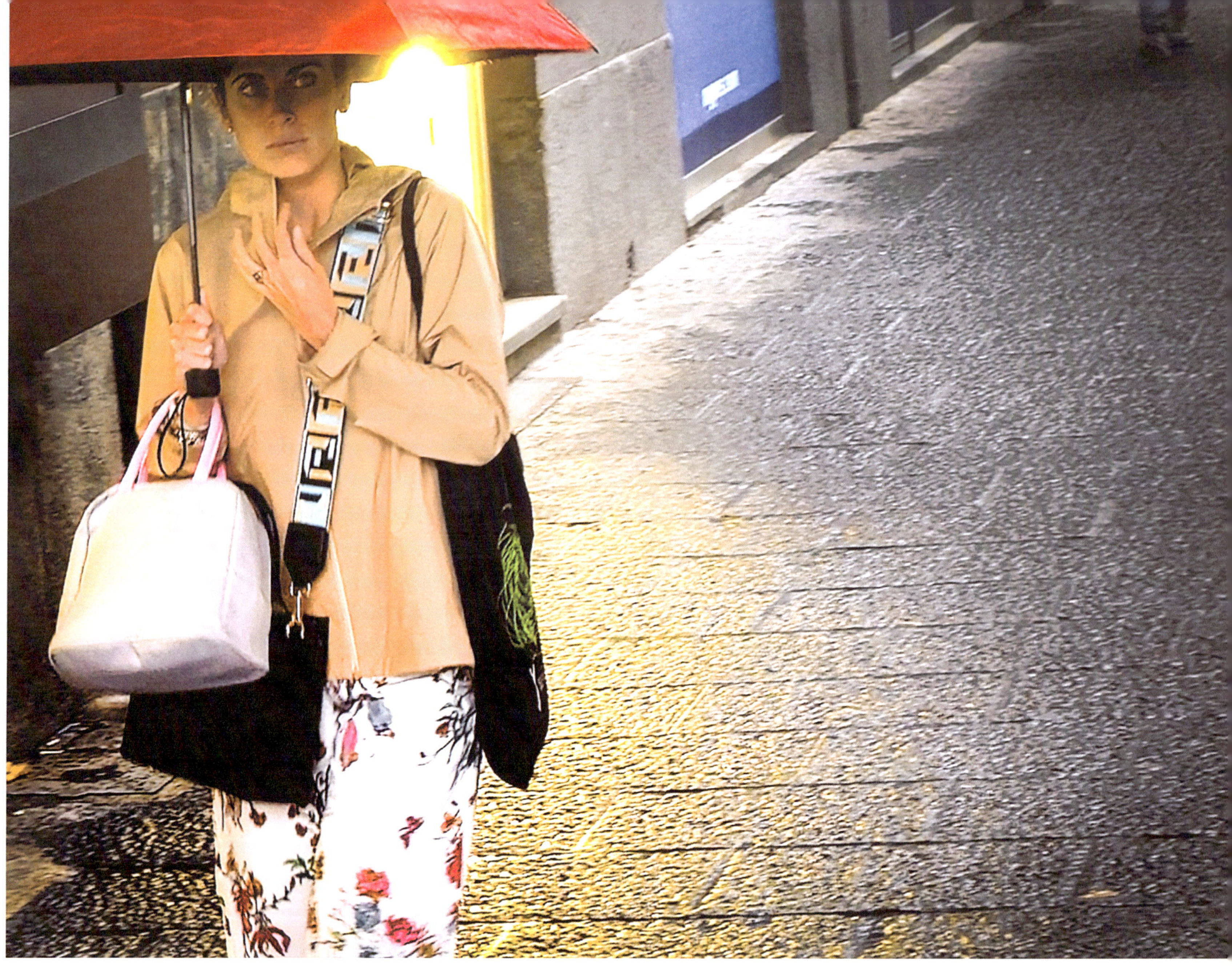

Rain Walk
Naples:
In the evening rain, a young woman walks cautiously, embracing the gentle drizzle in the graffiti covered streets of Naples.

Red Awning

Matera:

In this ancient city, crafted entirely with gray stone, a touch of color is like a visual oasis.

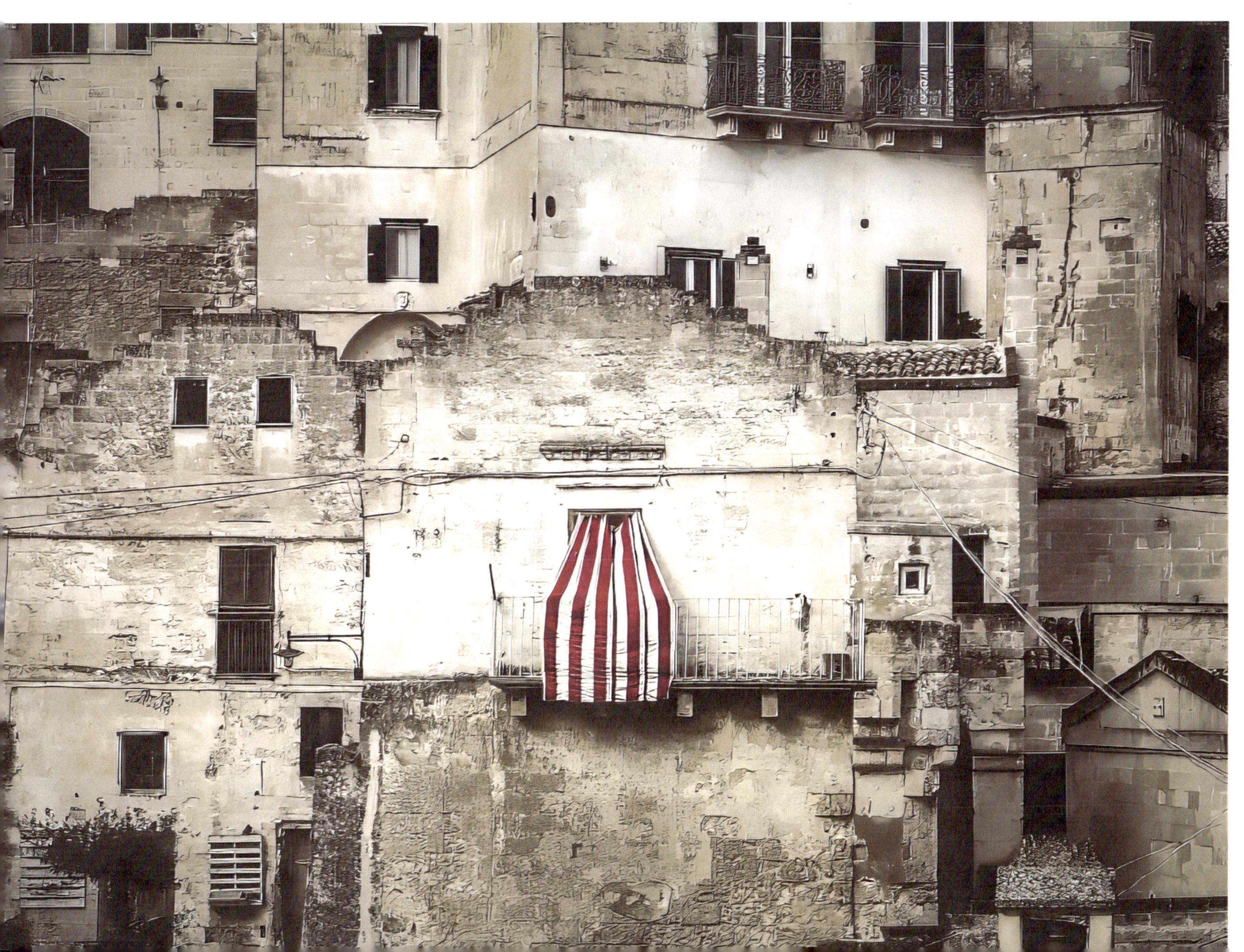

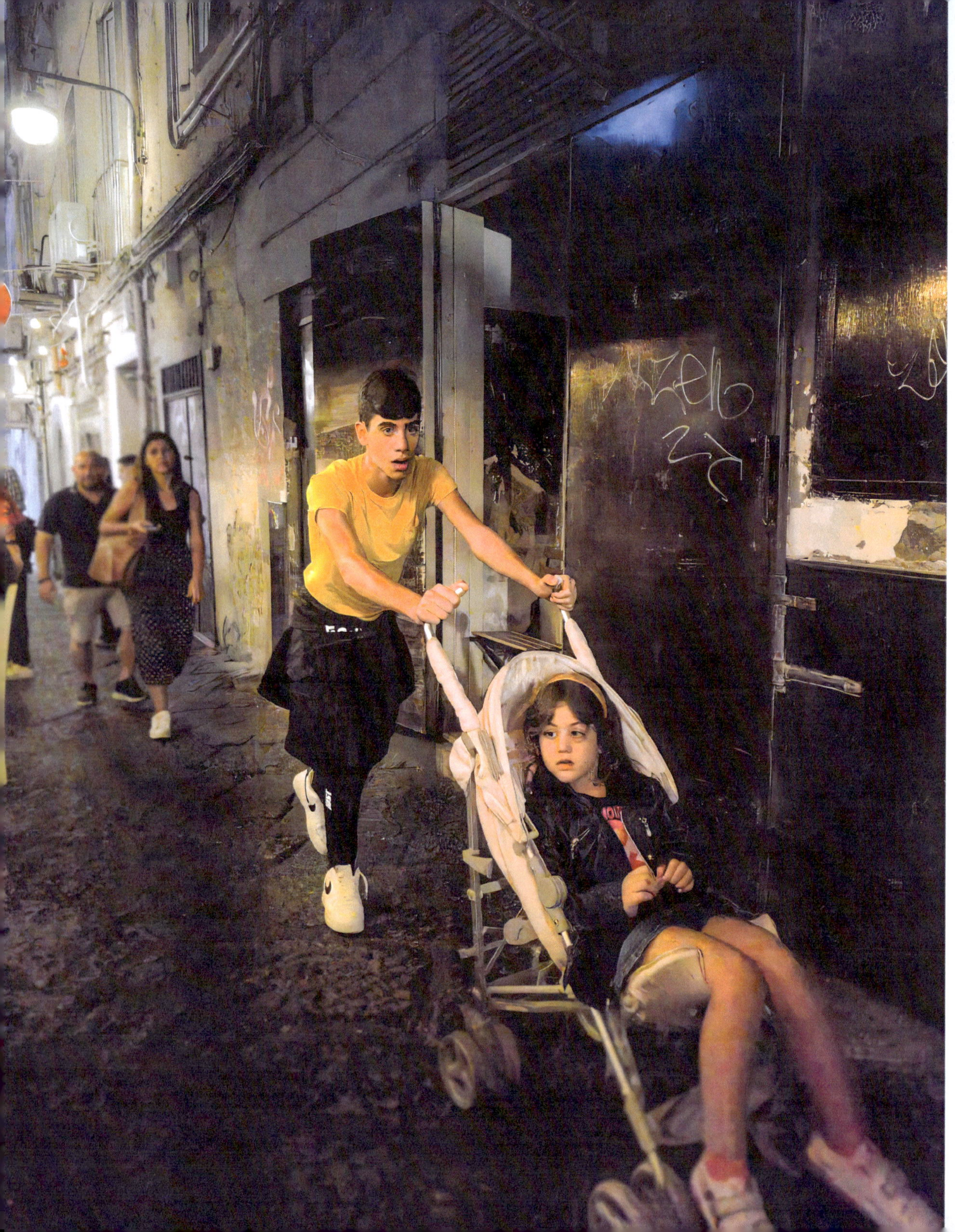

Passeggiata
Naples:
As in in most Italian cities, families and friends walk the early evening streets to mingle and catch up with one another..Old world social media..as it has been for hundreds of years.

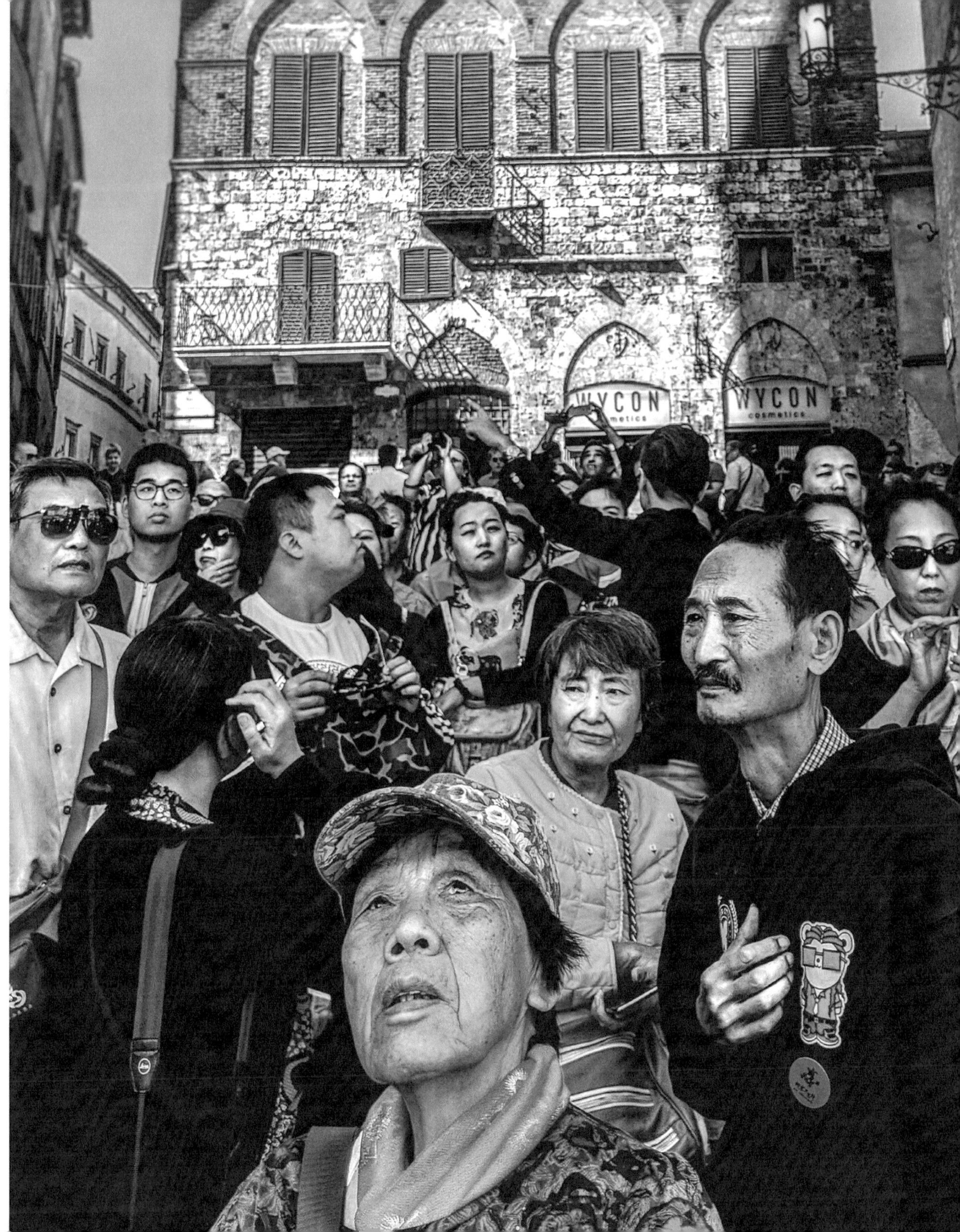

Asian Explorers
Siena:
A busload of Asian tourists arrive in Siena, marveling at the sights that unfold before them in this charming and historic city.

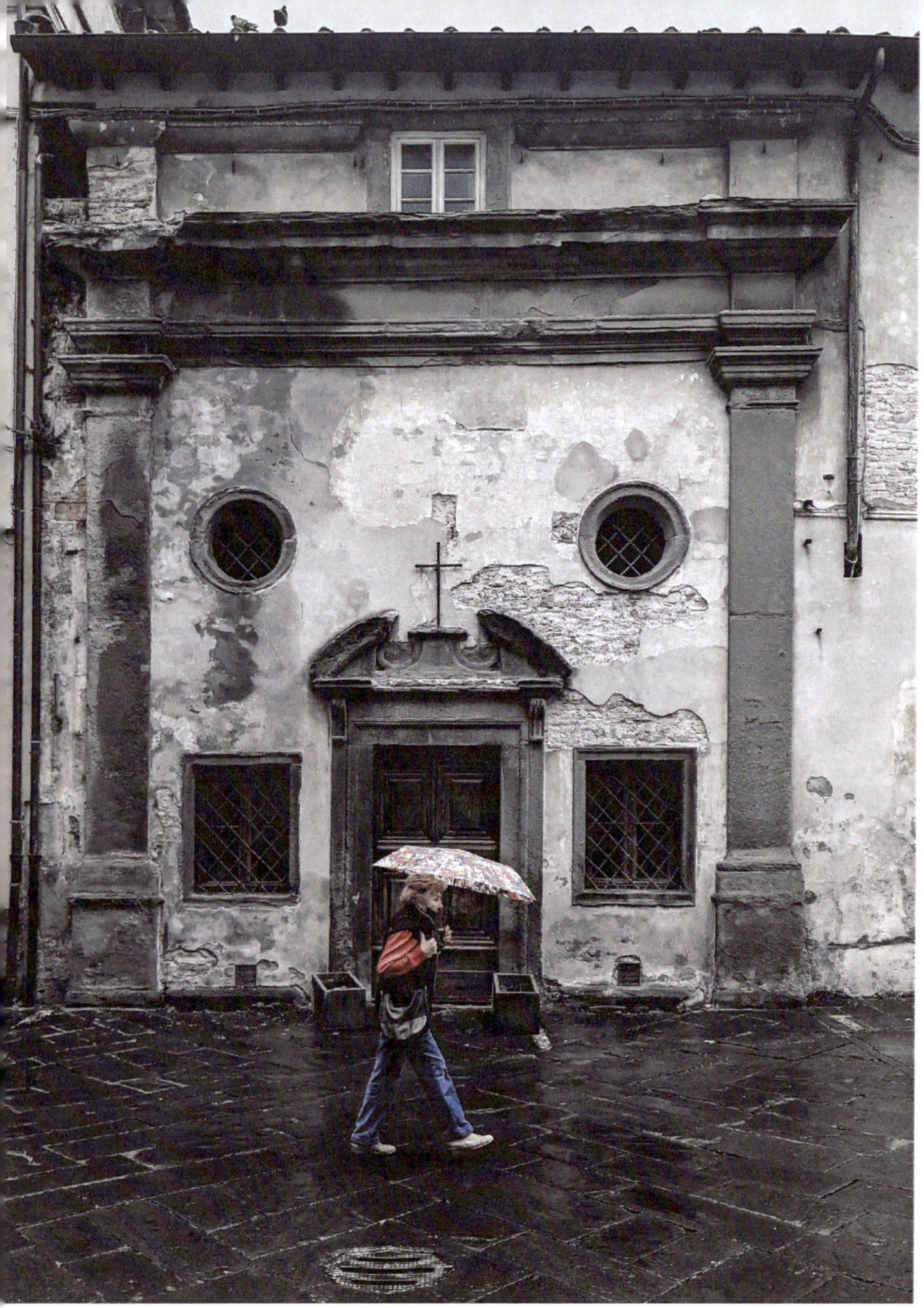

The Tourist
Anacapri:
This ancient setting embraces the modern as a photographer seeks
out images in the morning light.

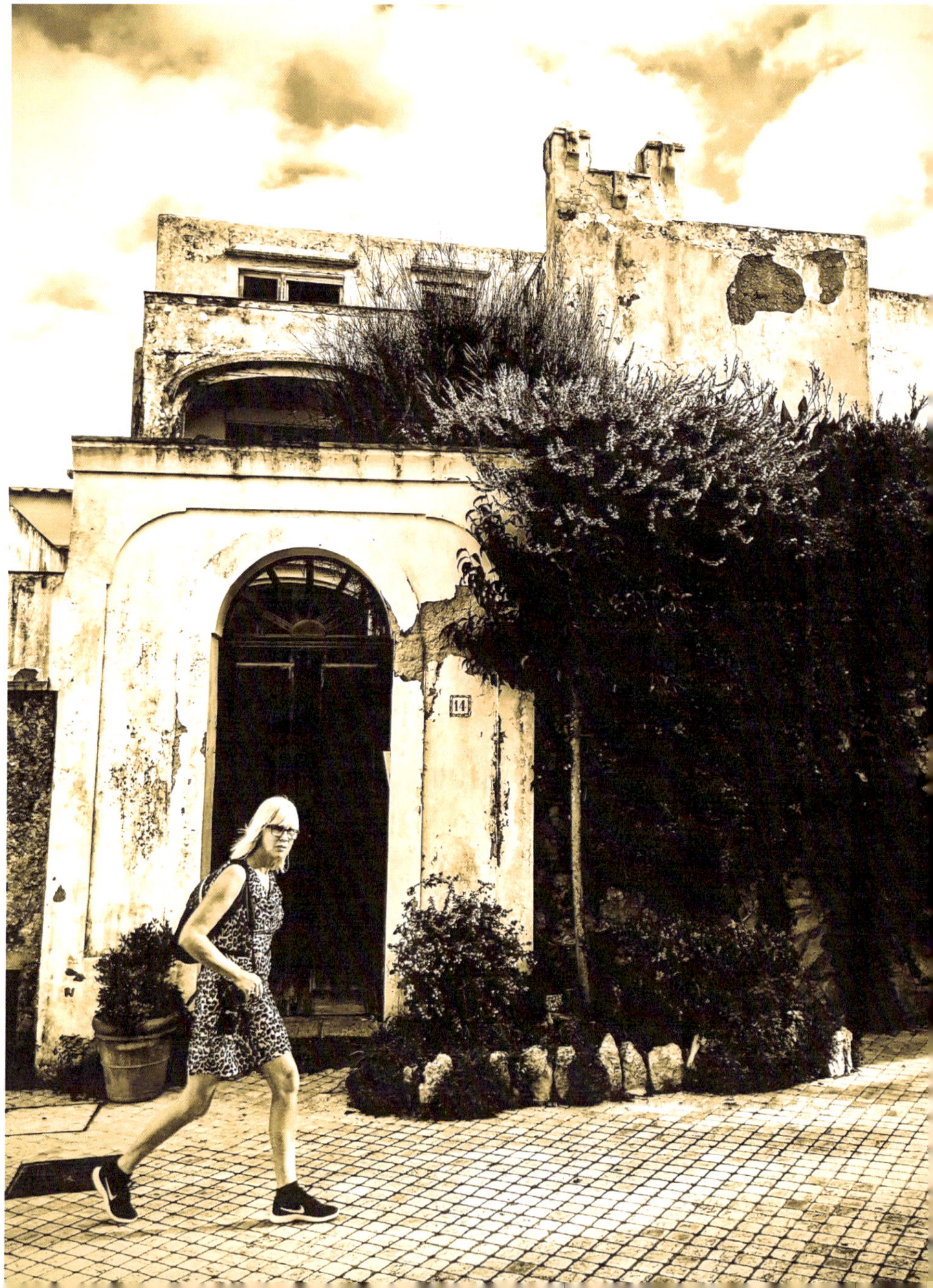

Rain Walker
Lucca:
A woman walks into the lines of a perfect composition as rain
cleanses the stone streets of Lucca.

Breath Me
Lucca:
Nearly completly enveloped in her boyfriends total embrace all that remains of her is her phone.

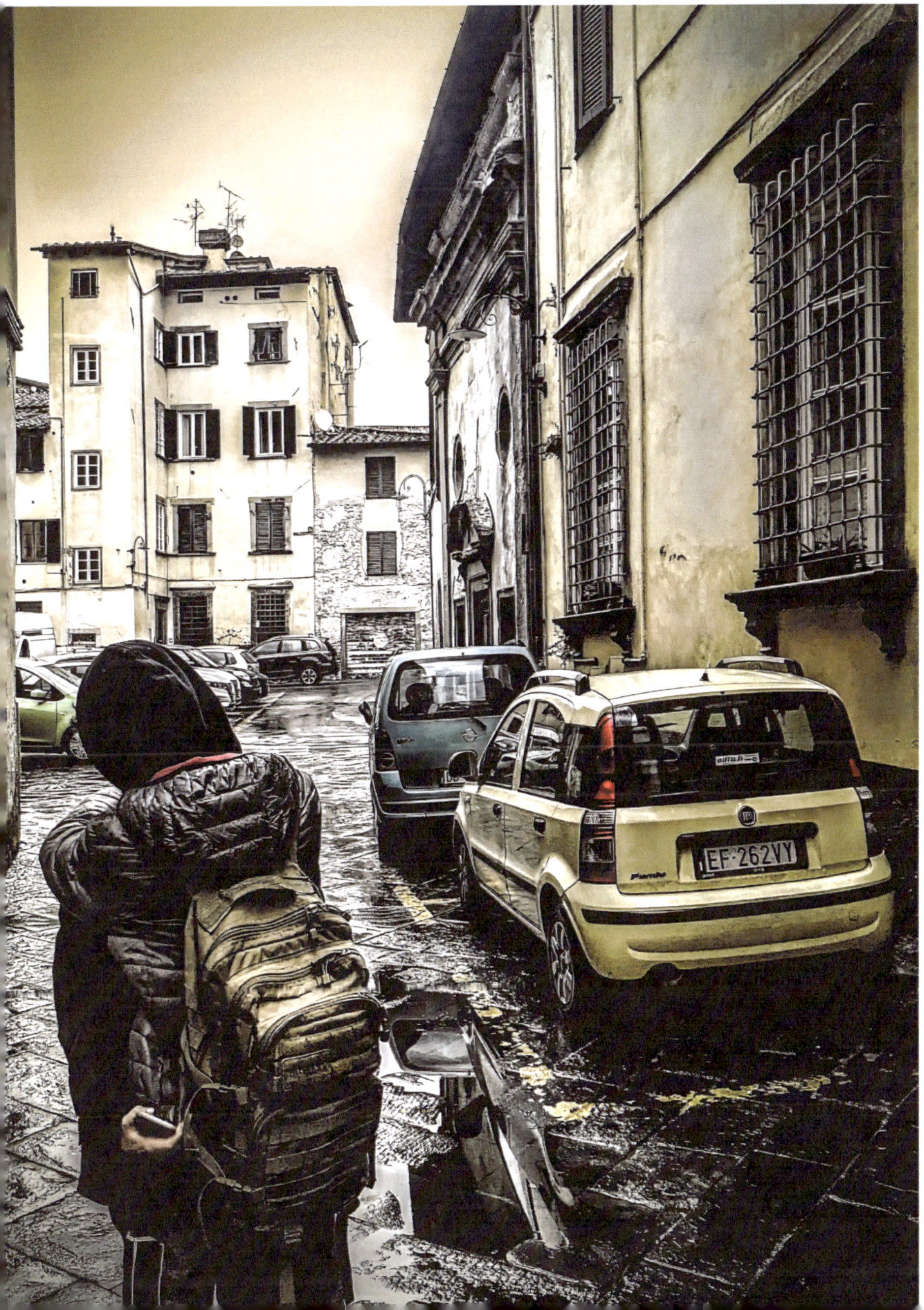

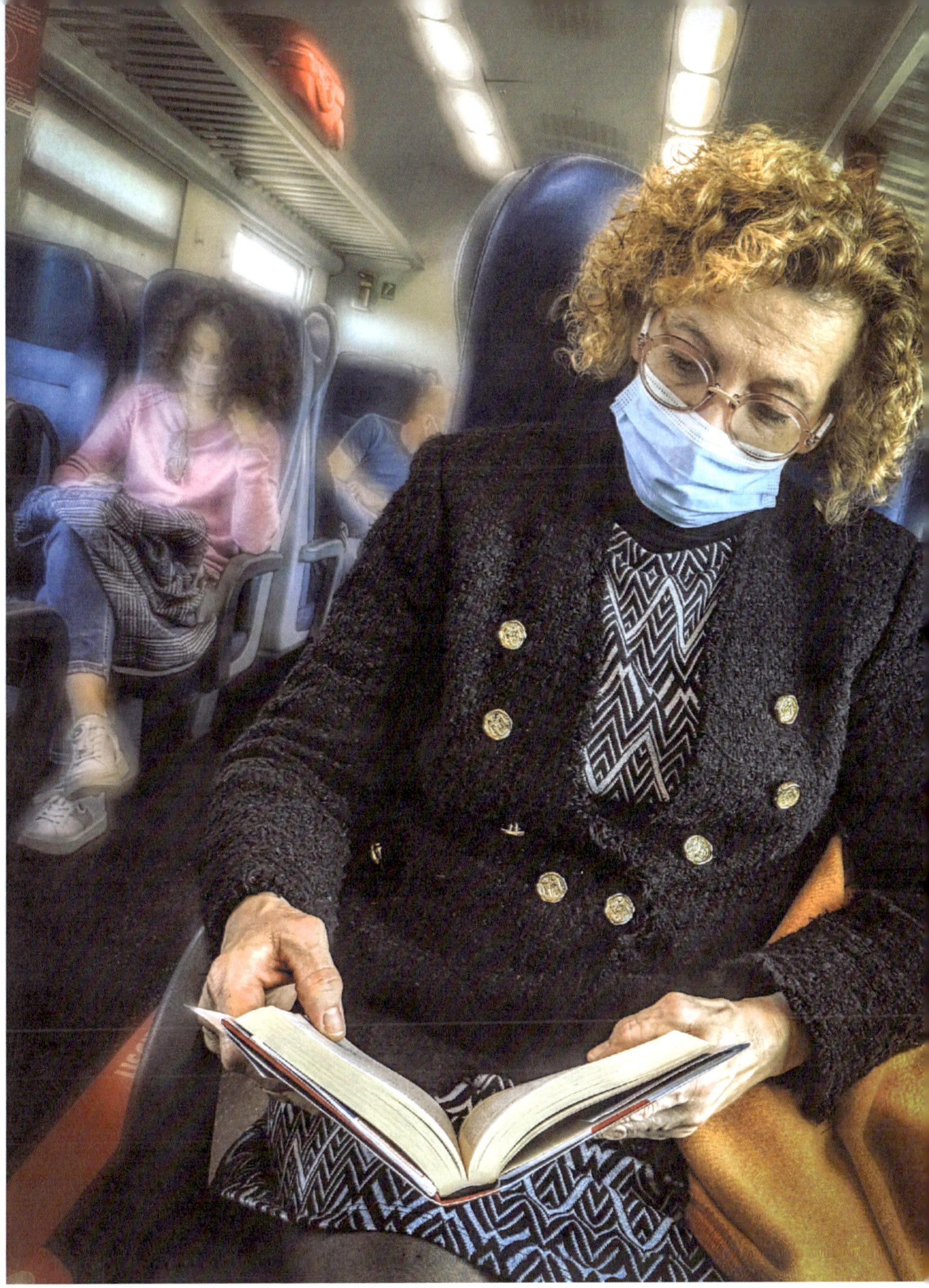

Train to Trieste
Trieste:
A passenger taking the morning train to work gets in a few more pages of her novel.

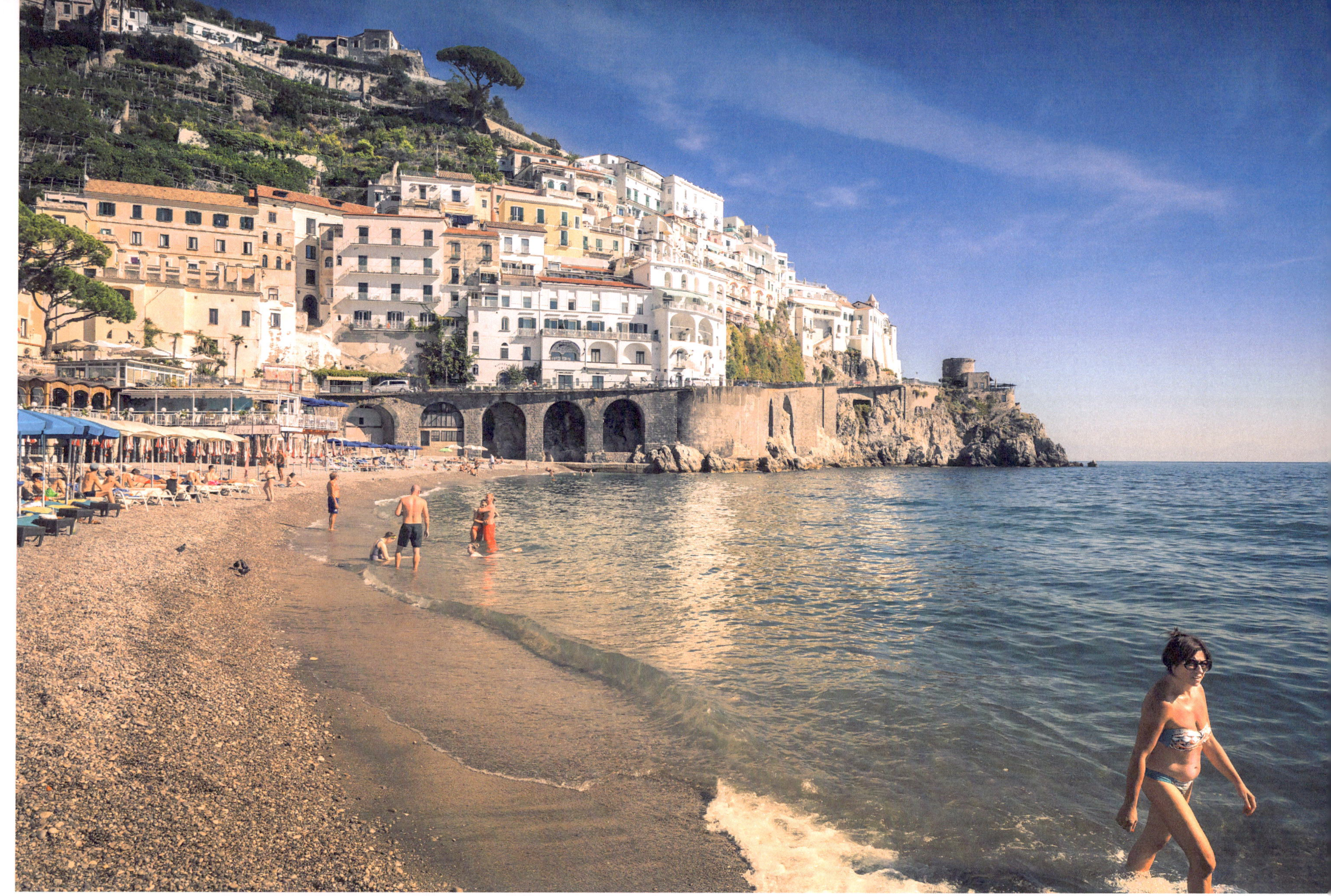

Fun in the Sun

Positano:

Against the backdrop of day drinkers, a woman power walks along the beach, blending fitness with the leisurely tourist atmosphere of the Amalfi Coast.

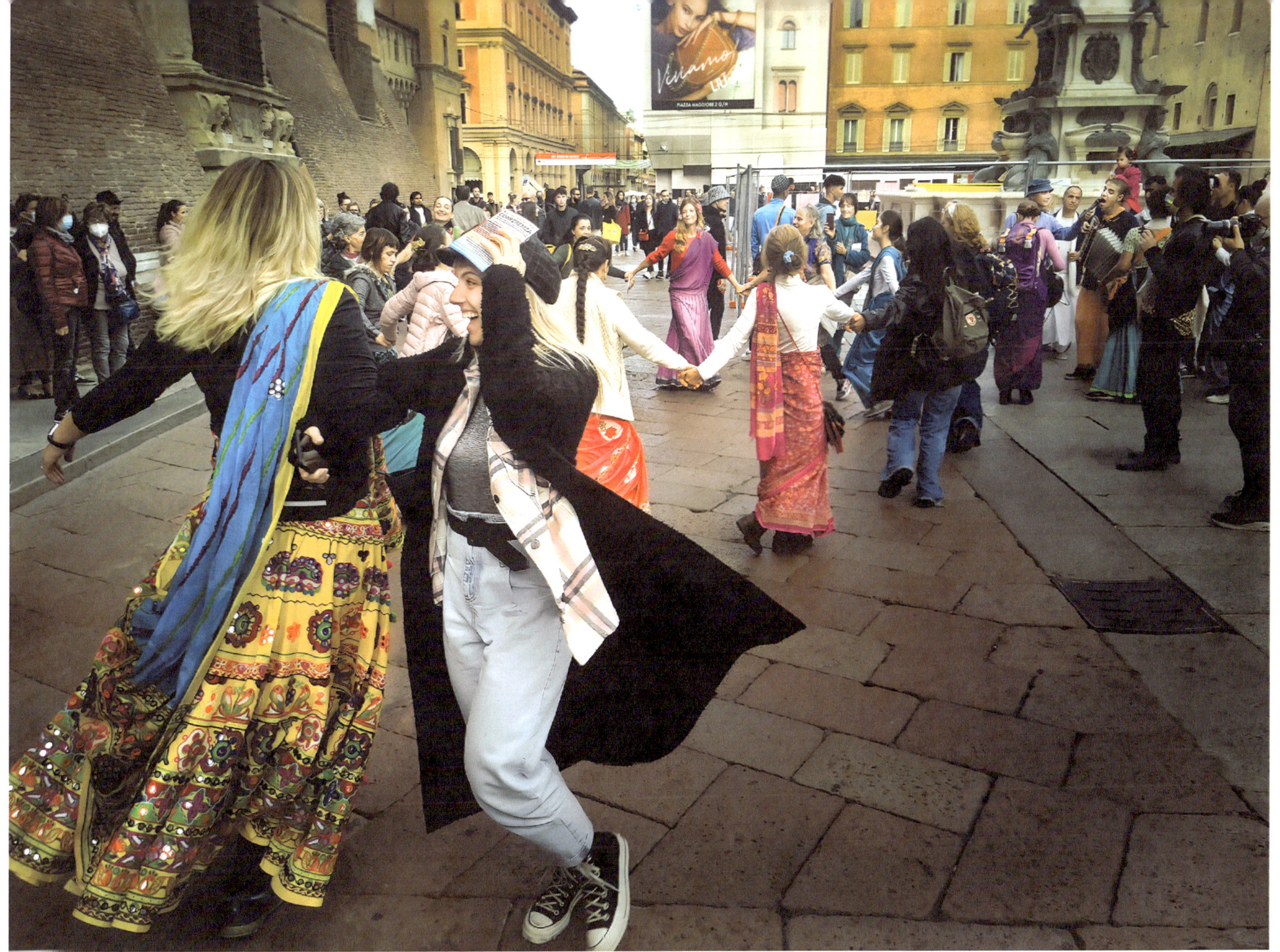

Spread the Love
Bologna:
A Hari Krishna group joyfully gathers tourists, sharing love and positive vibes with all in the heart of Bologna.

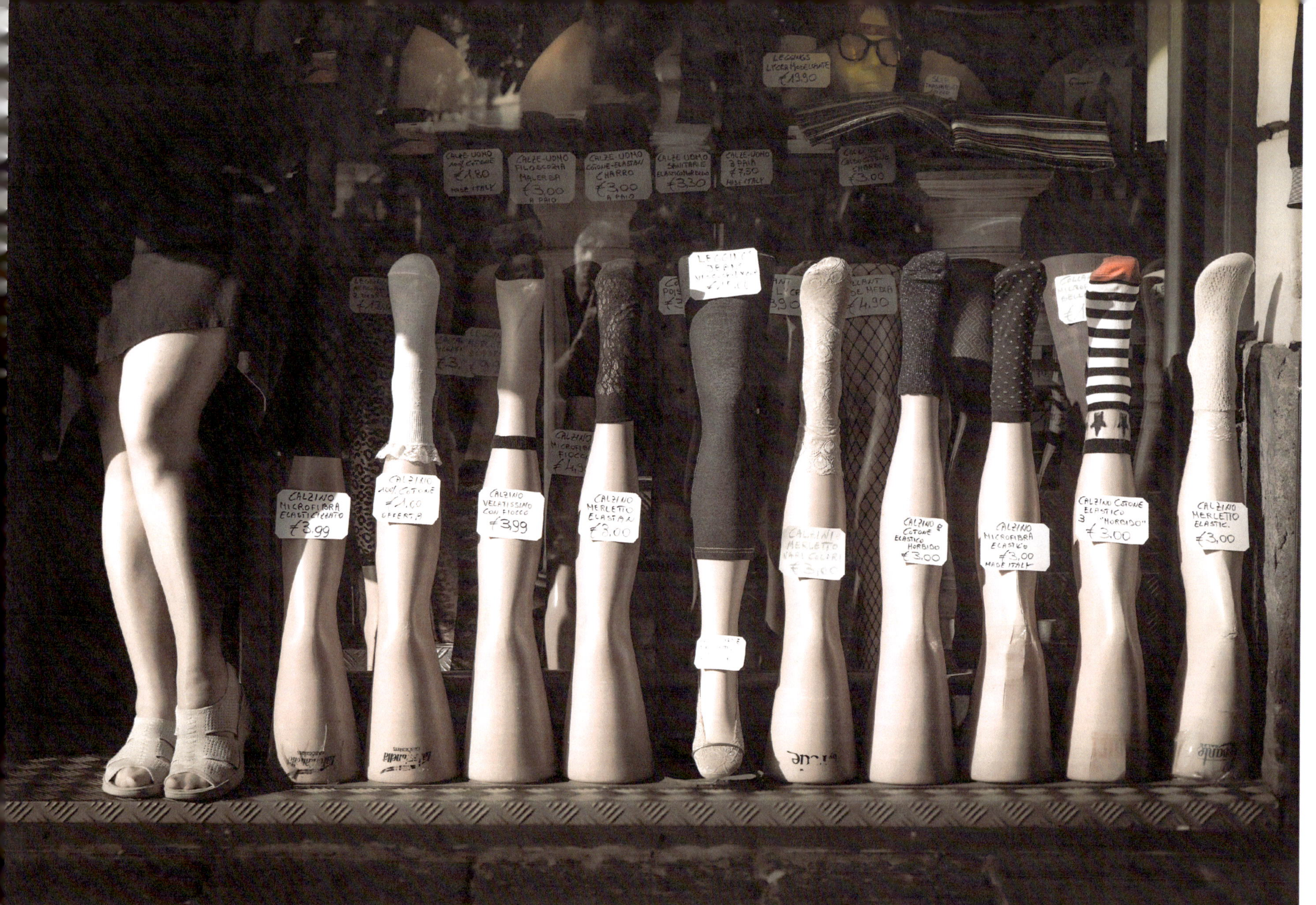

She's Got Legs
Catania:
A woman poses with mannequins in a lively street display, showcasing her new hosiery.

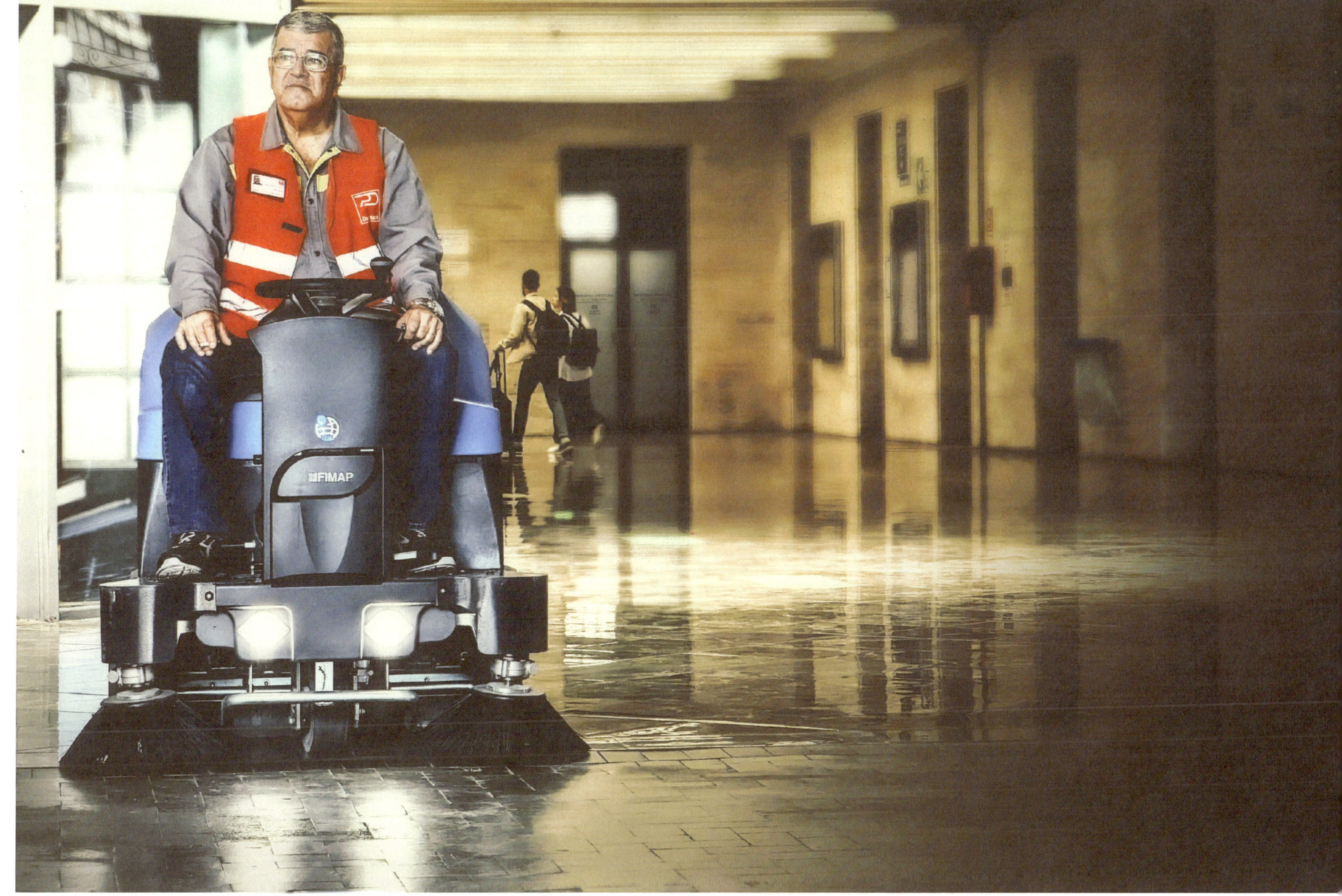

Sweeper
Palermo:
A janitor, lost in thought, rides the floor sweeper in the train station of Palermo, as his mind travels to another place and time.

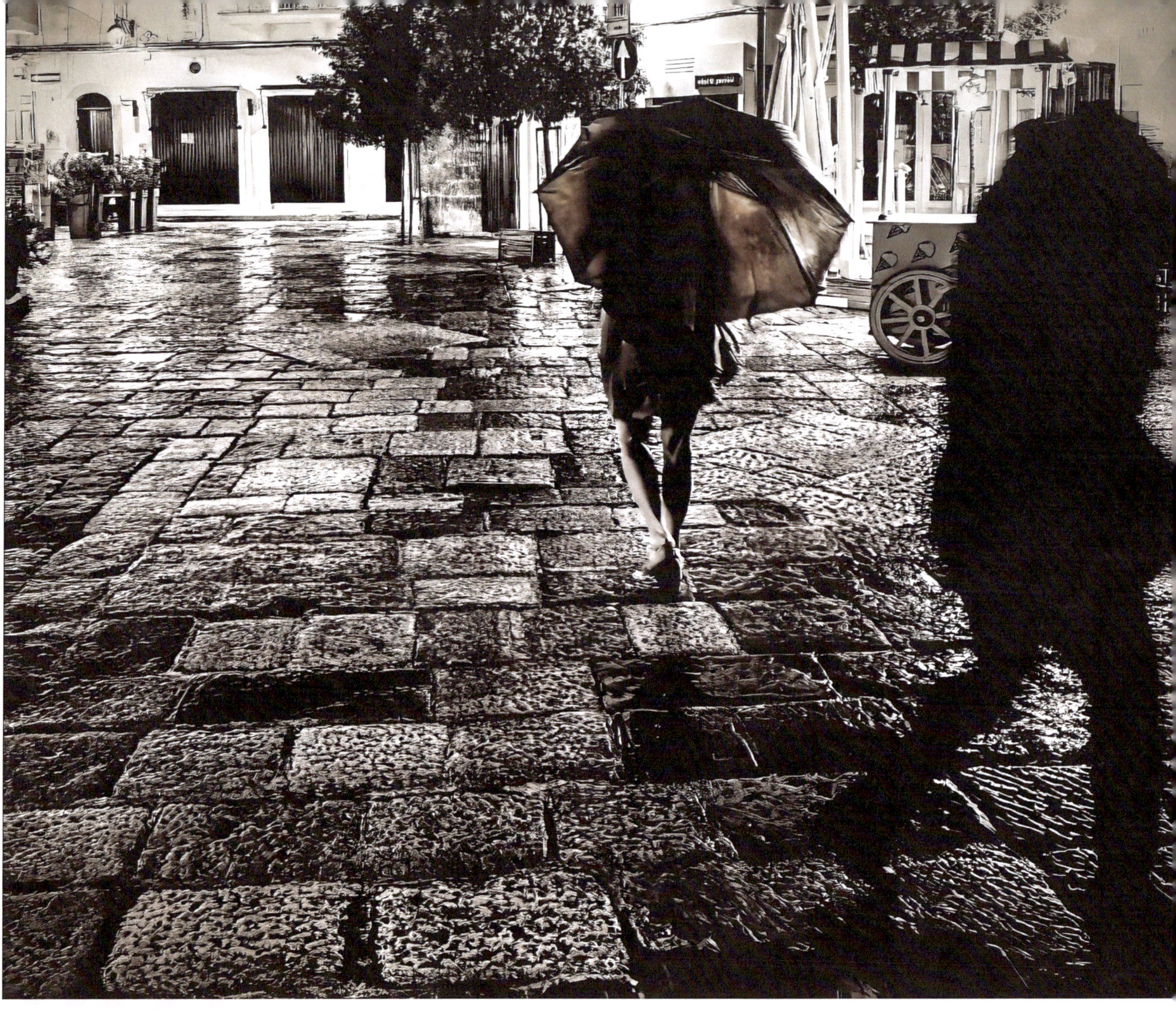

Evening Storm
Monopoli

A downpour in Monopoli washes away the steps of the day, cleansing the ancient stone streets.

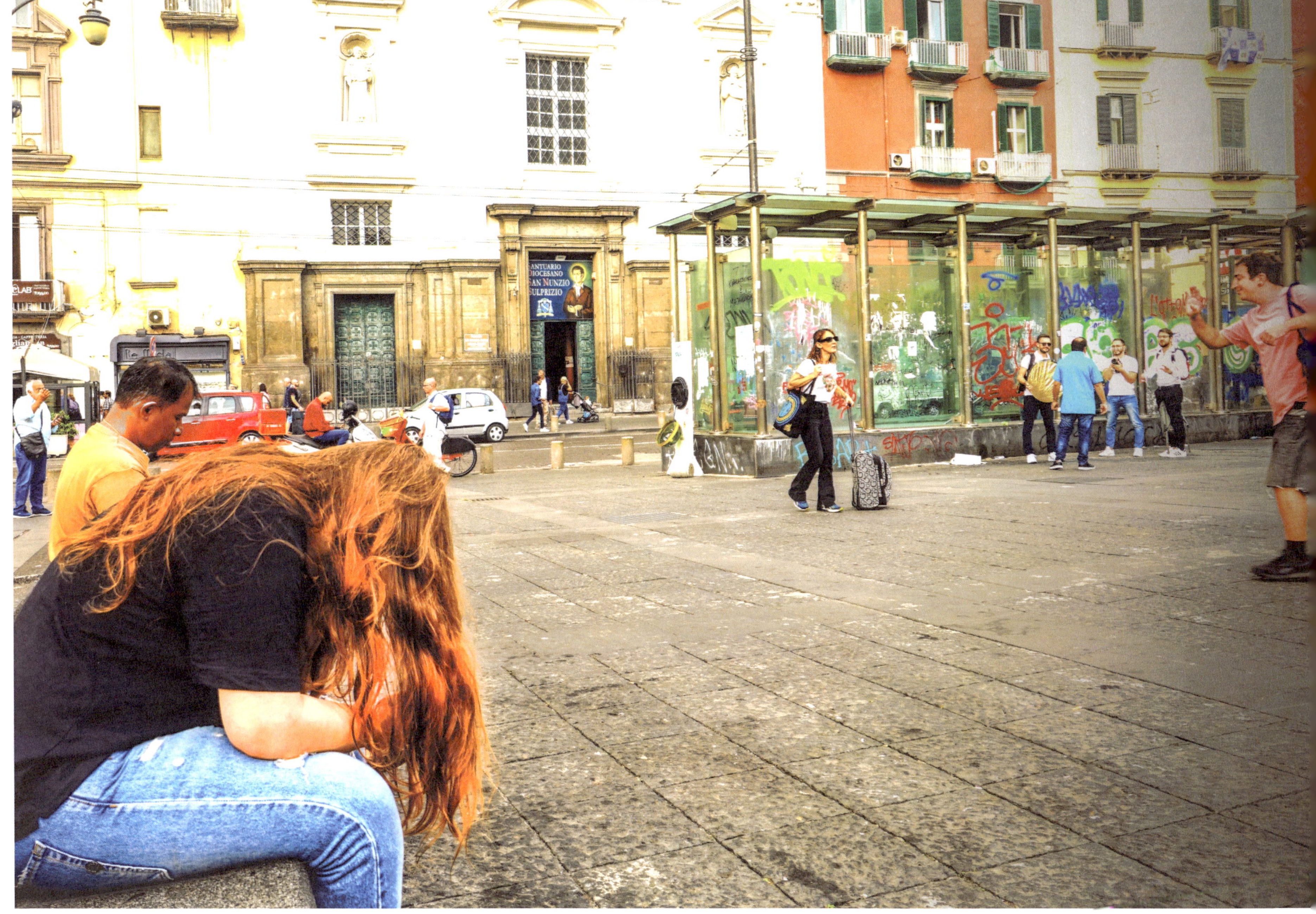

Radiant Redhead

Naples:

A girl with fire-red hair shields her phone from the sun, surrounded by others orbiting in their own worlds in the gritty city of Naples.

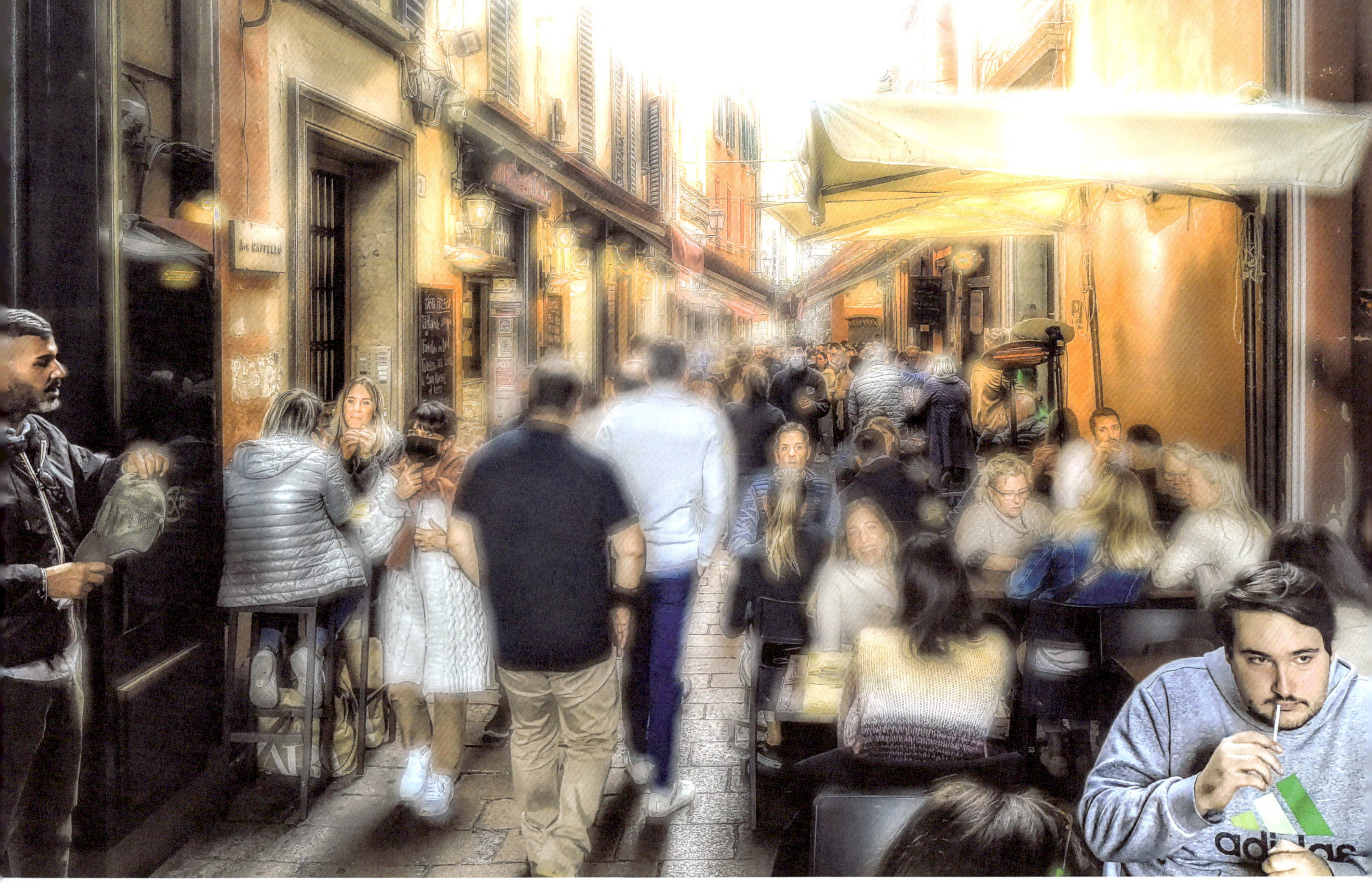

Lone Smoker
Bologna:
A suspicious local lights up after his lunch as thousands behind him laugh and dine. As far as the eye can see and on both sides there are hundreds of eateries...all packed.

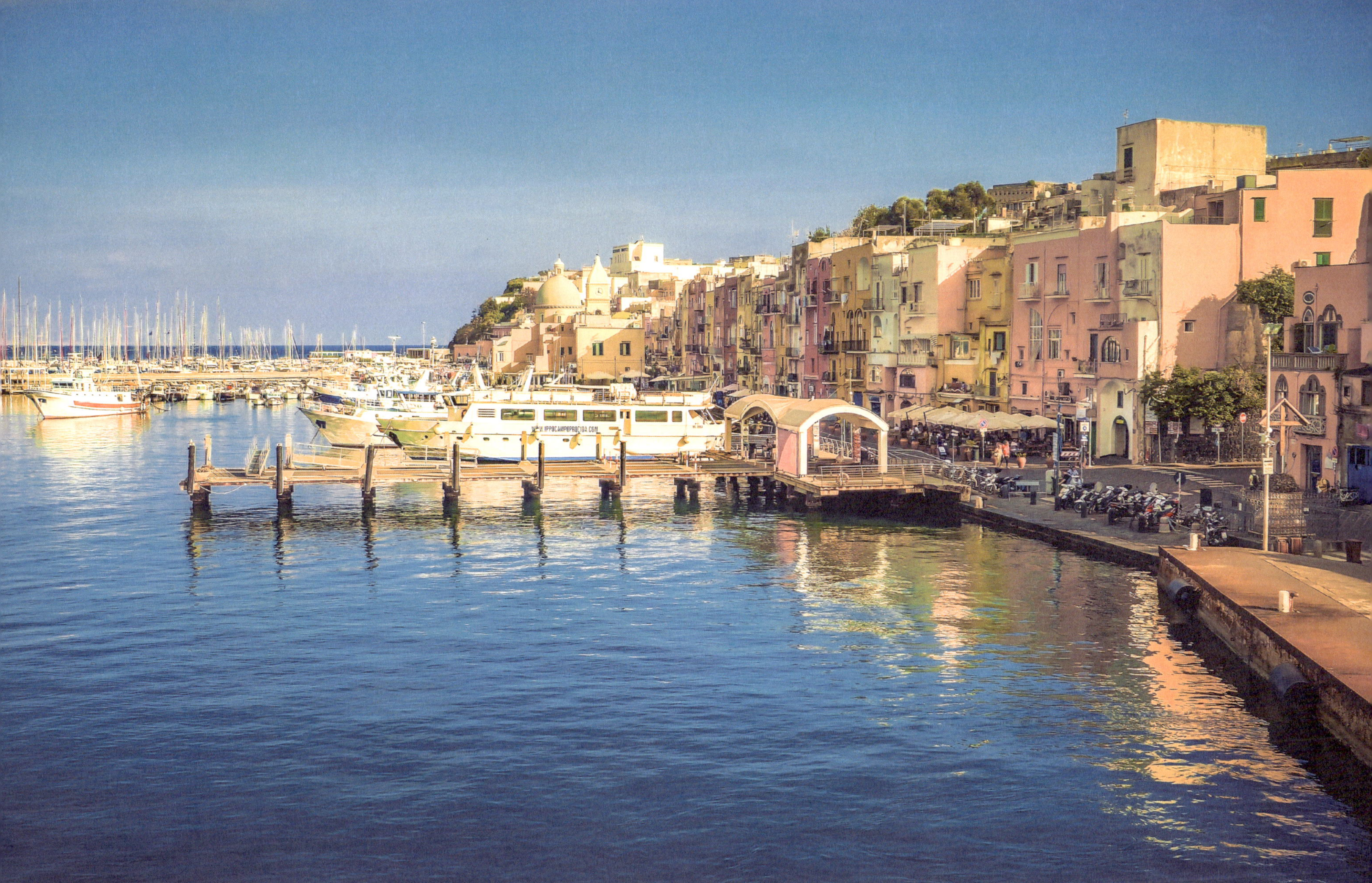

Another World
Procida:
Approaching the port of Procida. So beautiful is this island that all aboard cannot avert their gaze as if in disbelief that a place so magnificent really exists.

Arrival
Naples:
Out of the loud chaotic city into
the quiet dark comfort of his hotel,
a traveler arrives at a converted
old monastery.

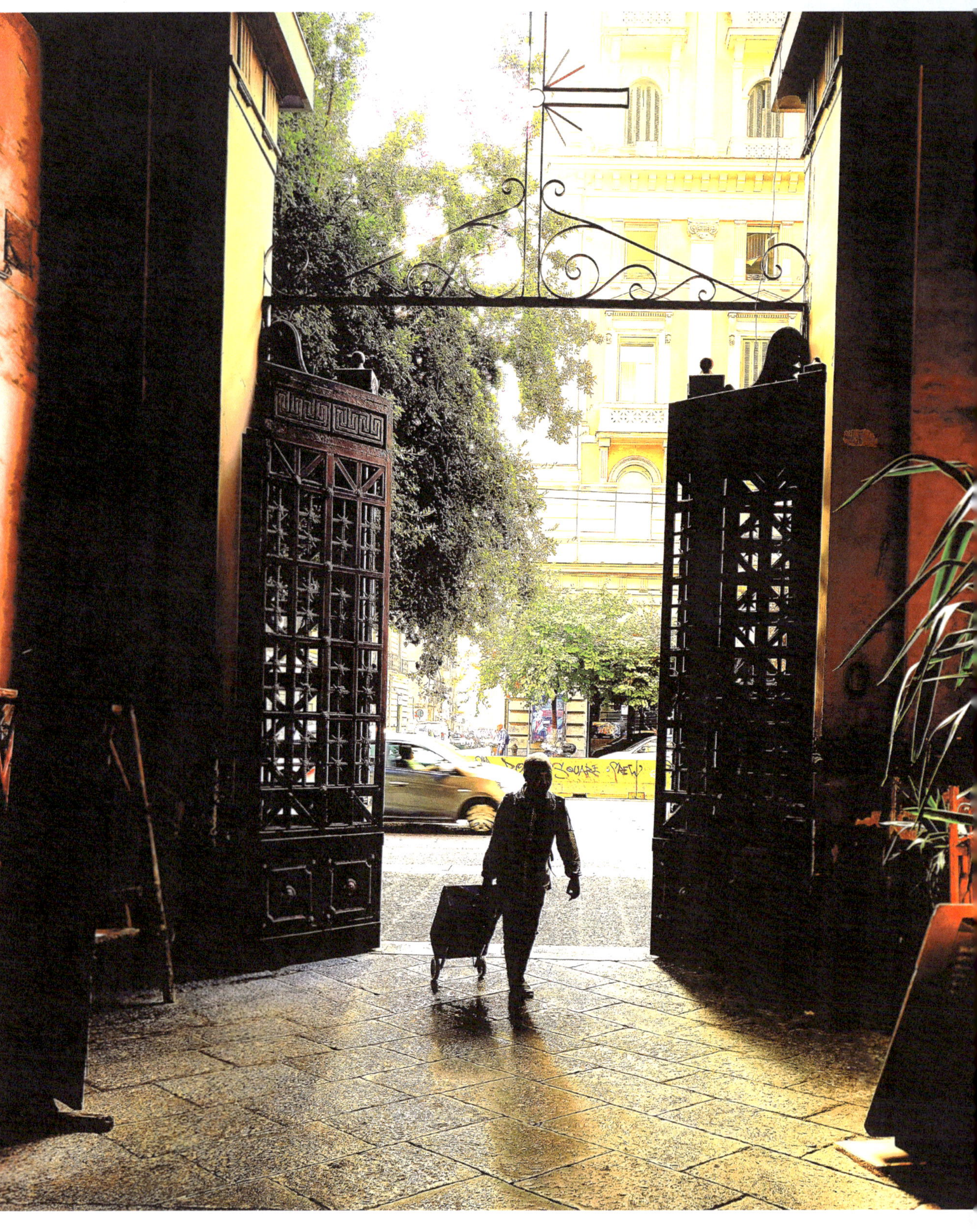

Train To Trieste
Trieste:
An older woman catches the atten-
tion of her boarding friend. They
will spend the short journey
laughing and talking, friends since
childhood.

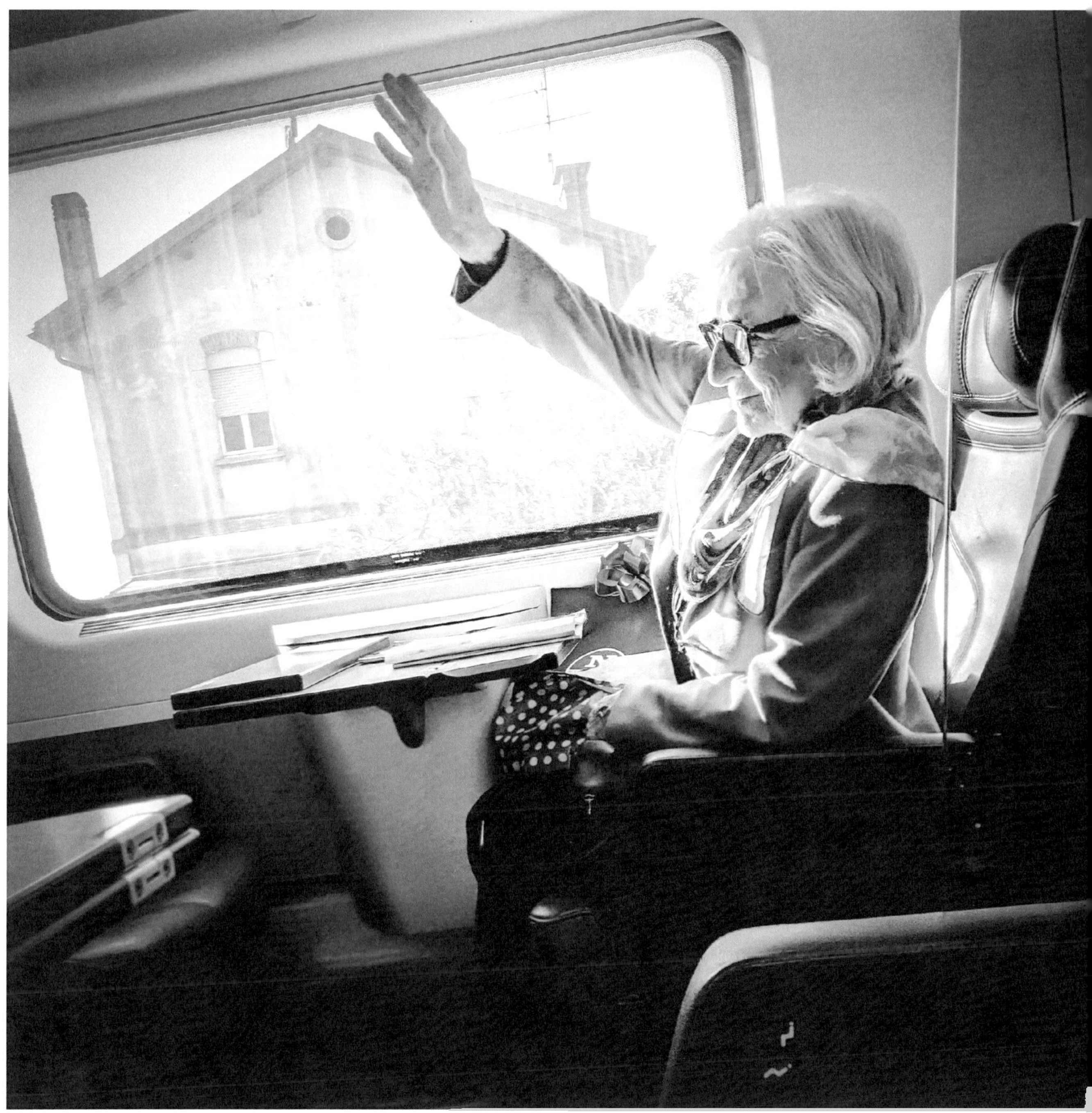

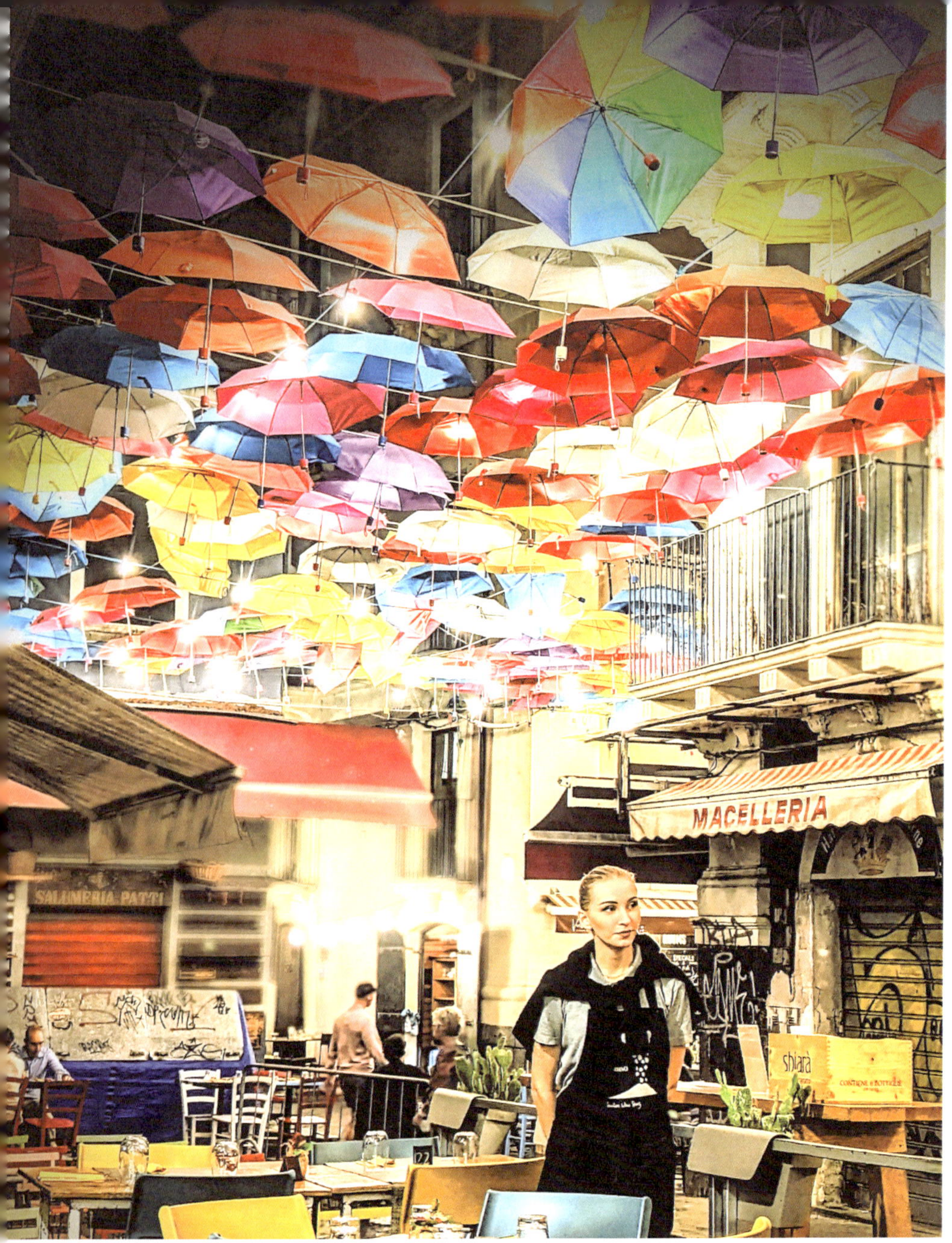

Maria
Catania:
Thoughts drift to her family in Russia as this immigrant server awaits the evening patrons. Italian with a Russian accent has an interesting vibe!

Balloon Pilot
Catania:
A peddler floats his wares down the middle of a street while texting his wife...nothing unusual about that.

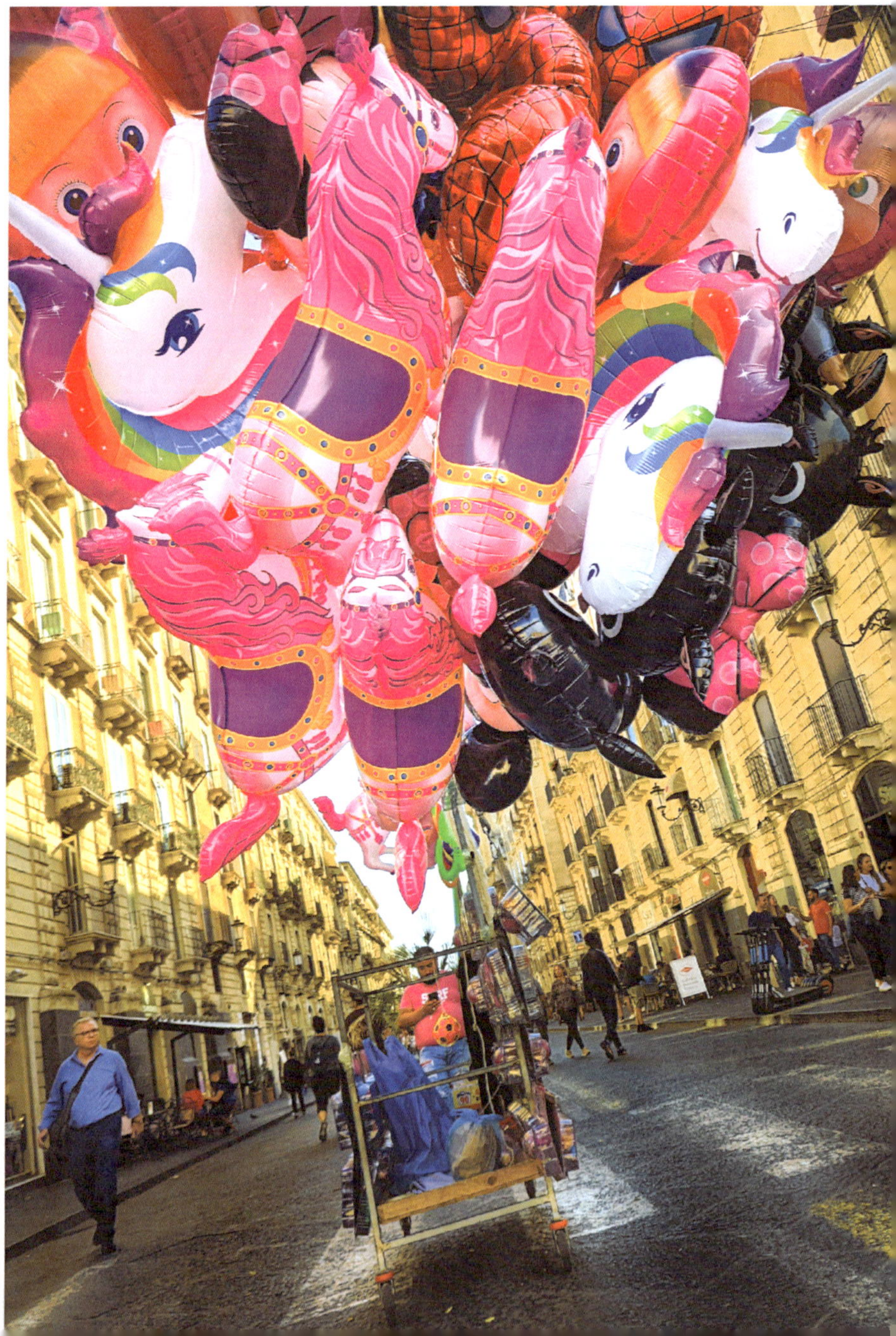

Stop
Naples:
A nun rushes towards me, faster than I can run away. She explained that she was giving a few euros to the poor behind her then asked me to pray for them with her.

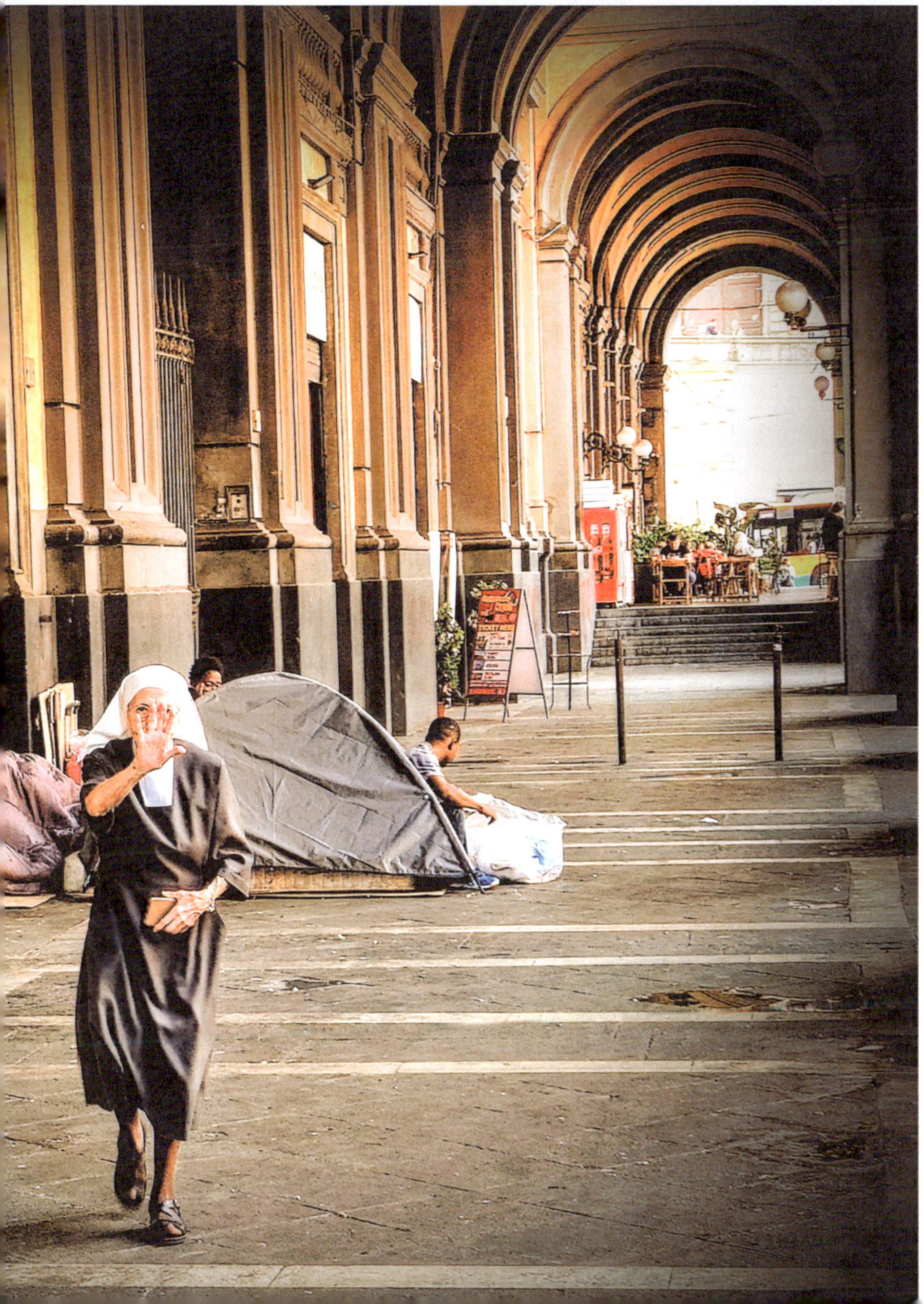

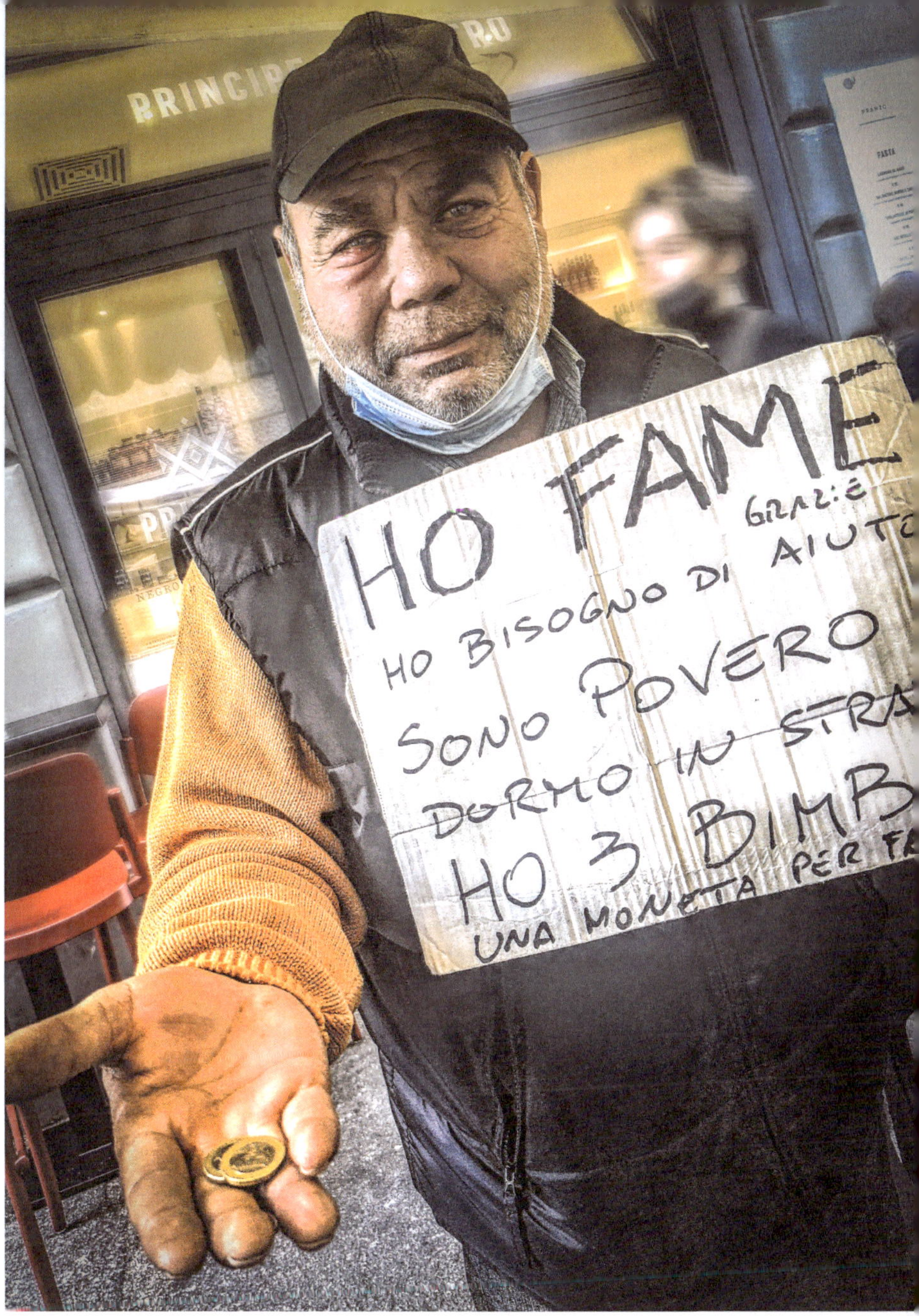

I Am Hungry
Bologna:
In the gastronomic capital of Italy ironically many hungry walk the streets.

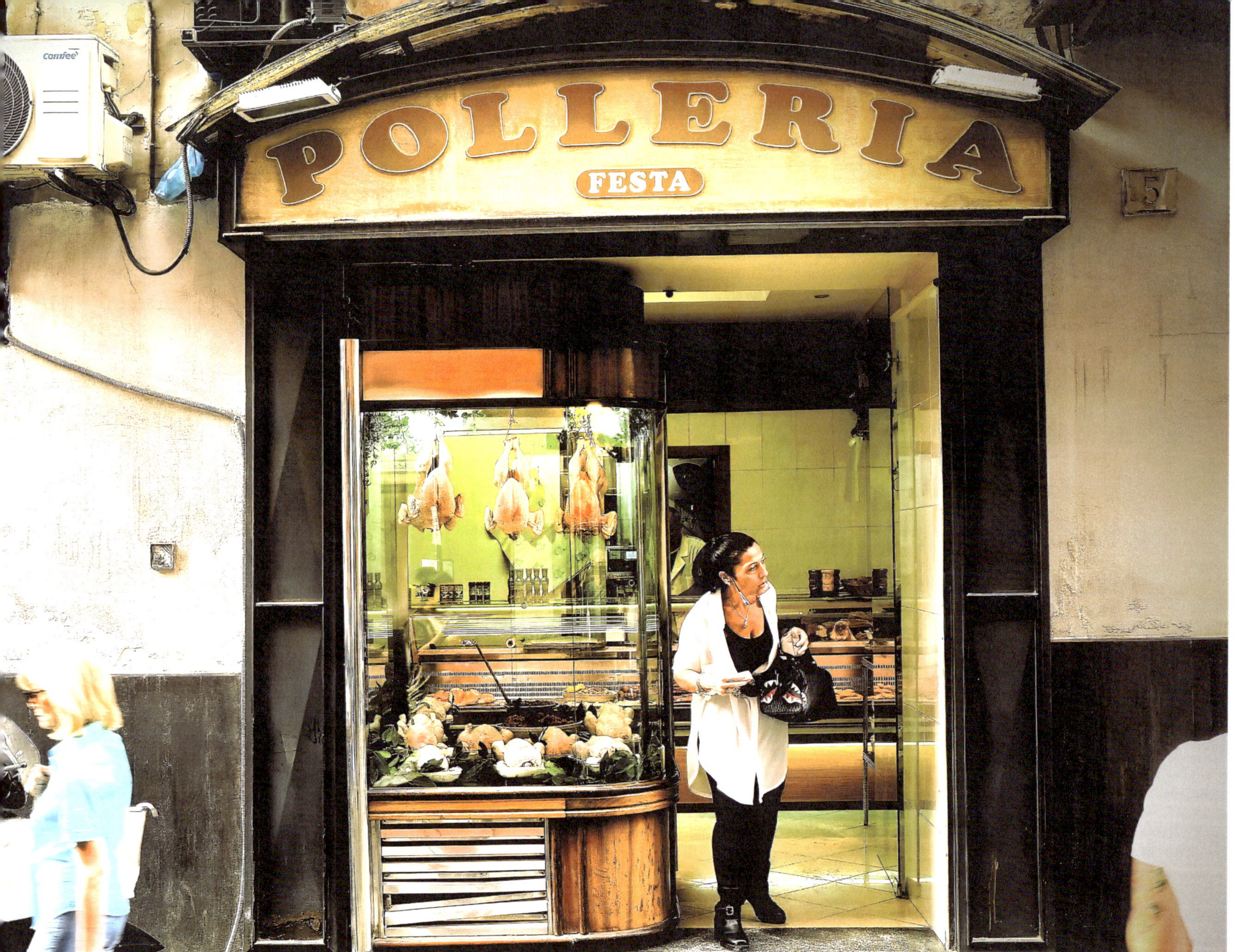

Poultry Shop
Naples:
A woman with a shark purse, calls out for her daughter while selecting the evening dinner in the lively markets of Naples.

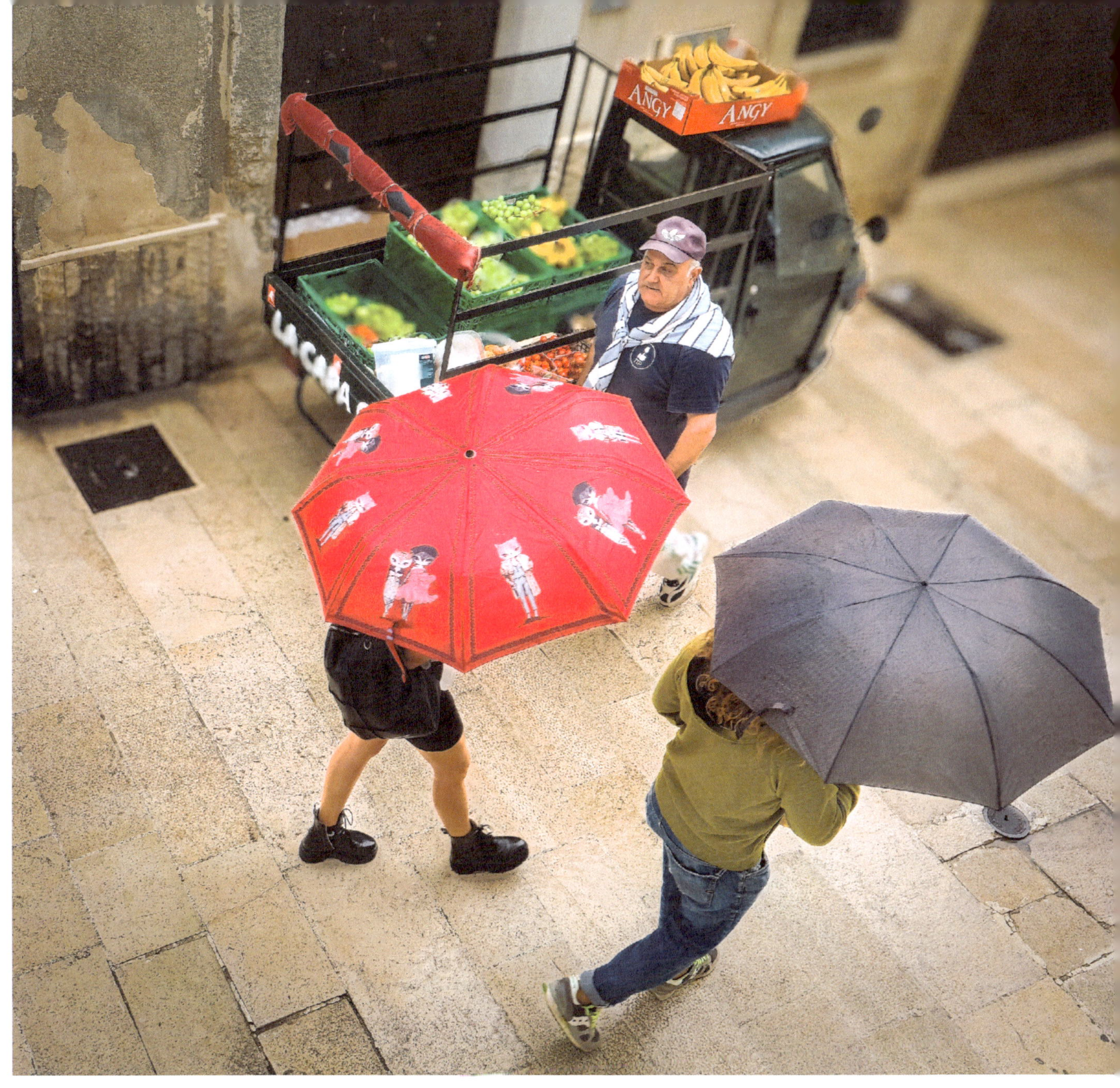

Fruit Man
Monopoli:
A rain filled day in Monopoli brings few sales to this street vendor.
But there will always be tomorrow...

Morning Routine

Trieste:
In a local cafe, the morning papers are perused just like every other day, as Trieste begins its daily rhythm.

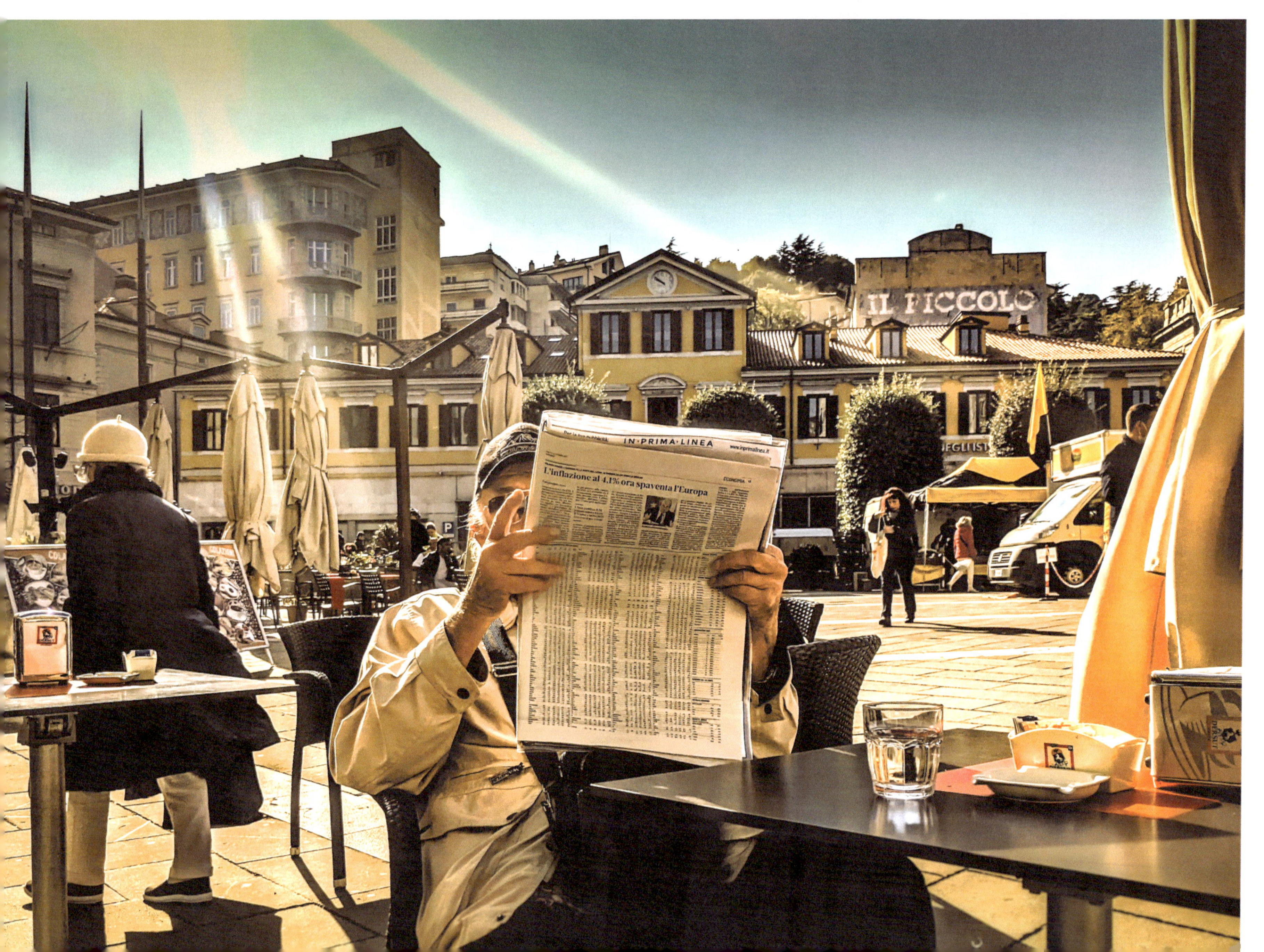

Hot Nonnas
Bari:
Nonnas adorned in winter clothing on this warm evening, gather on their favorite bench, in the same spot, a nightly tradition.

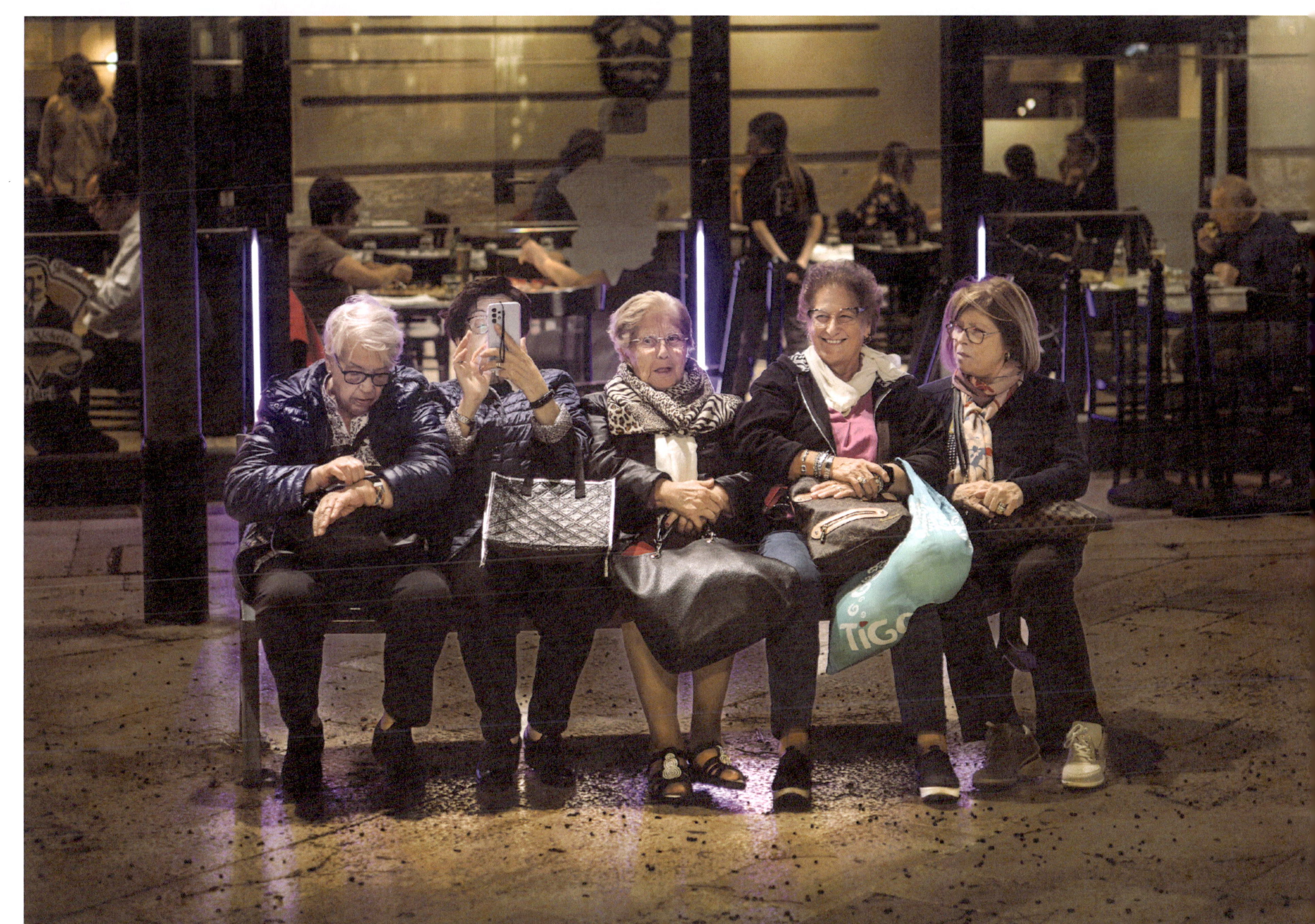

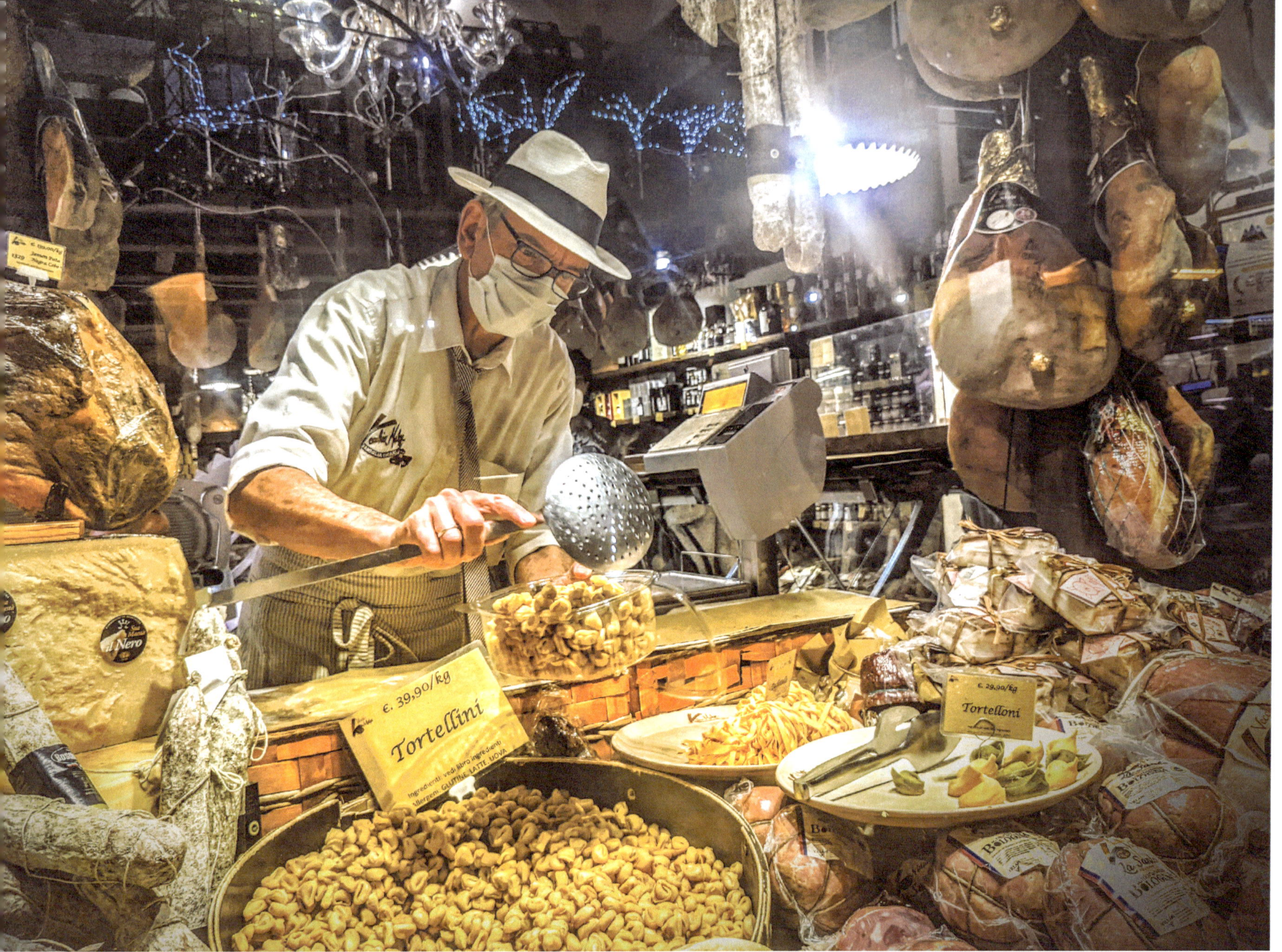

Pasta Paradise

Bologna:

Tortellini, scooped by this pasta vendor, flourishes in this city renowned for its delectable bolognese. Actually the locals say the town is most known for Mortadella...which is amazing!

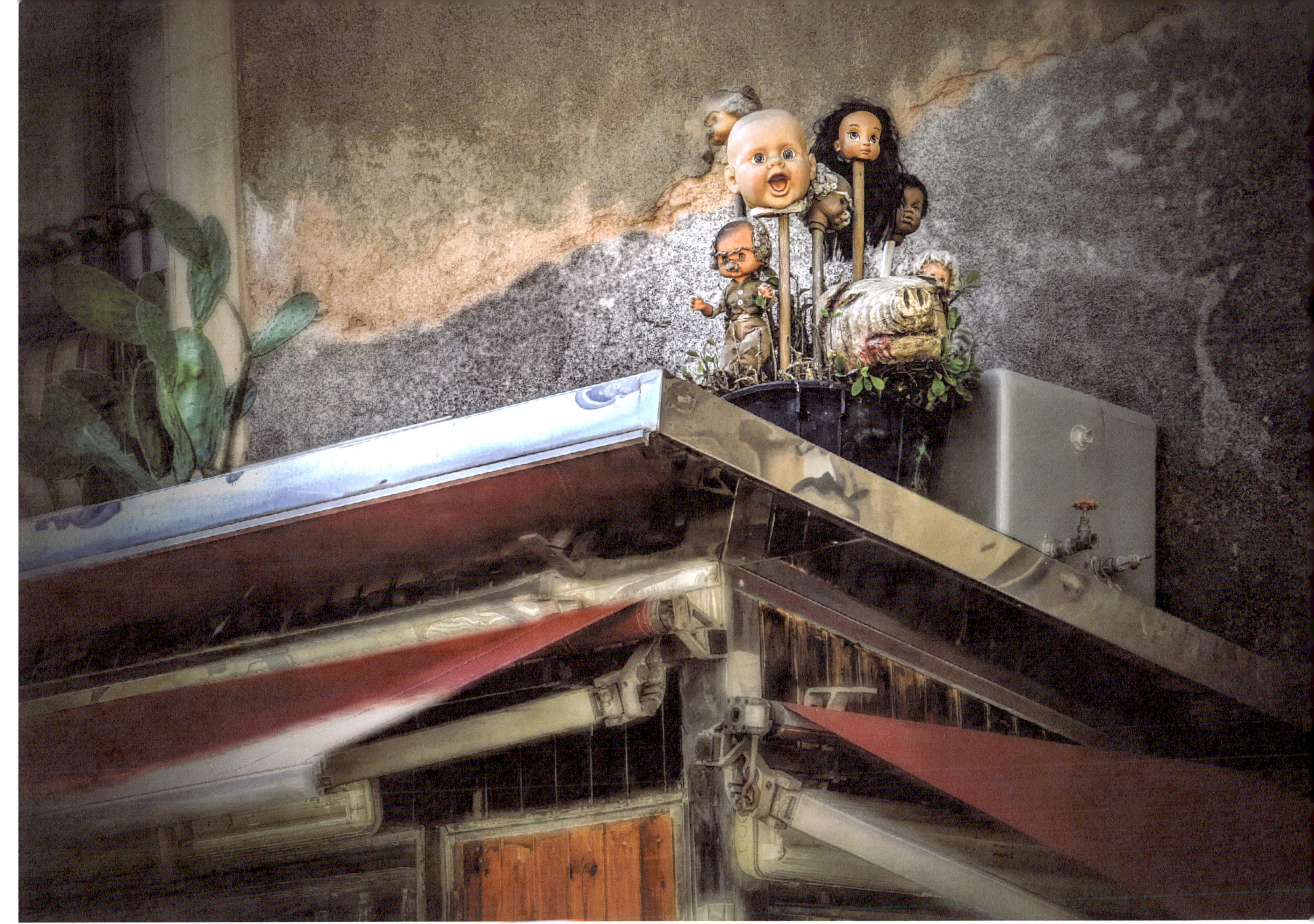

Enigmatic Charms
Catania:
Unsure of its meaning, but cautious not to enter – Catania casts intriguing spells. Religion and superstition so curiously blended as one in southern Italy.

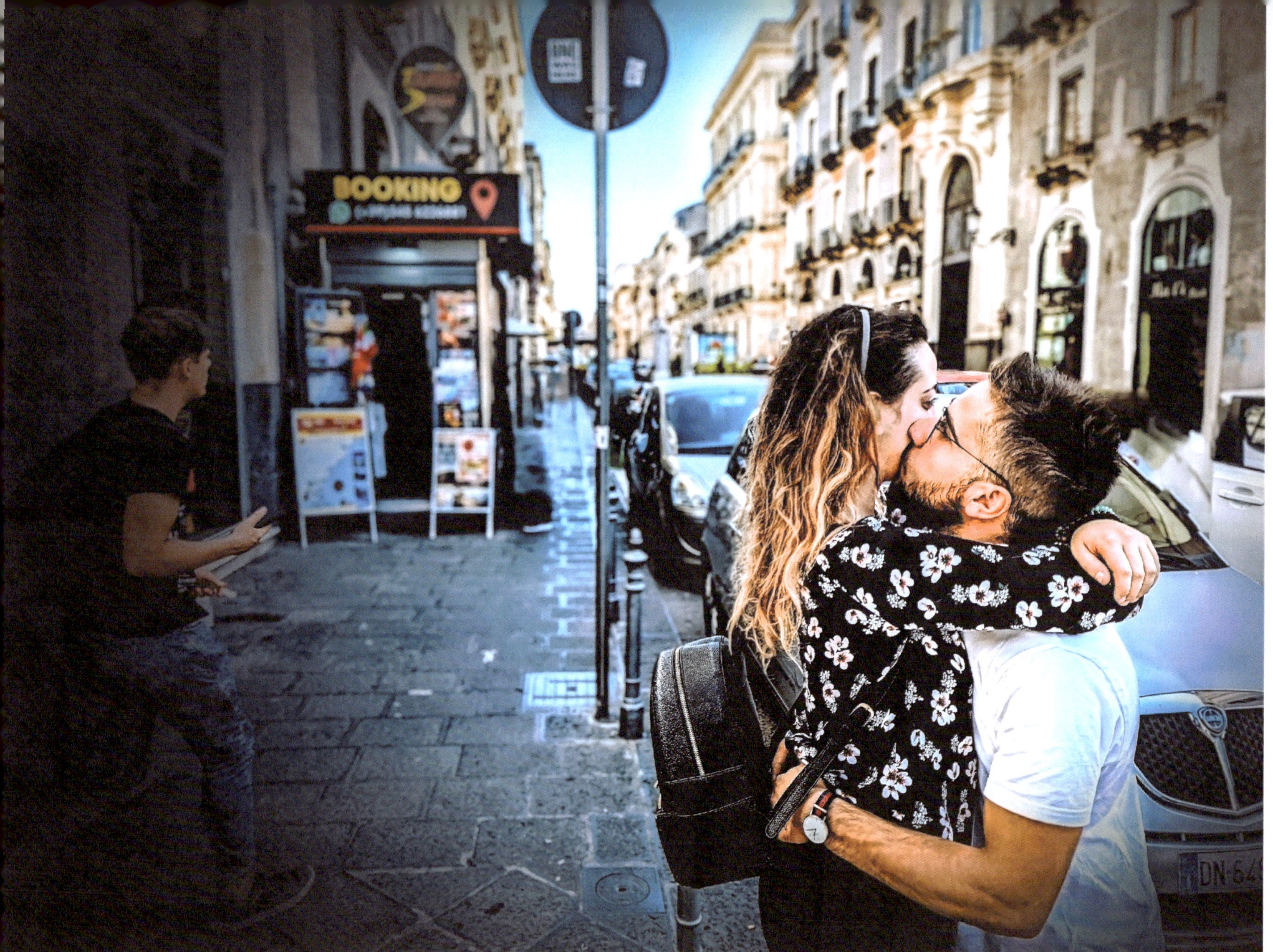

Just Kiss Me
Catania:
A young girl reluctantly gives in to her boyfriends apologies in this embrace on the gritty streets of Catania. Love in one form or another is a common sight in this emotionally charged country.

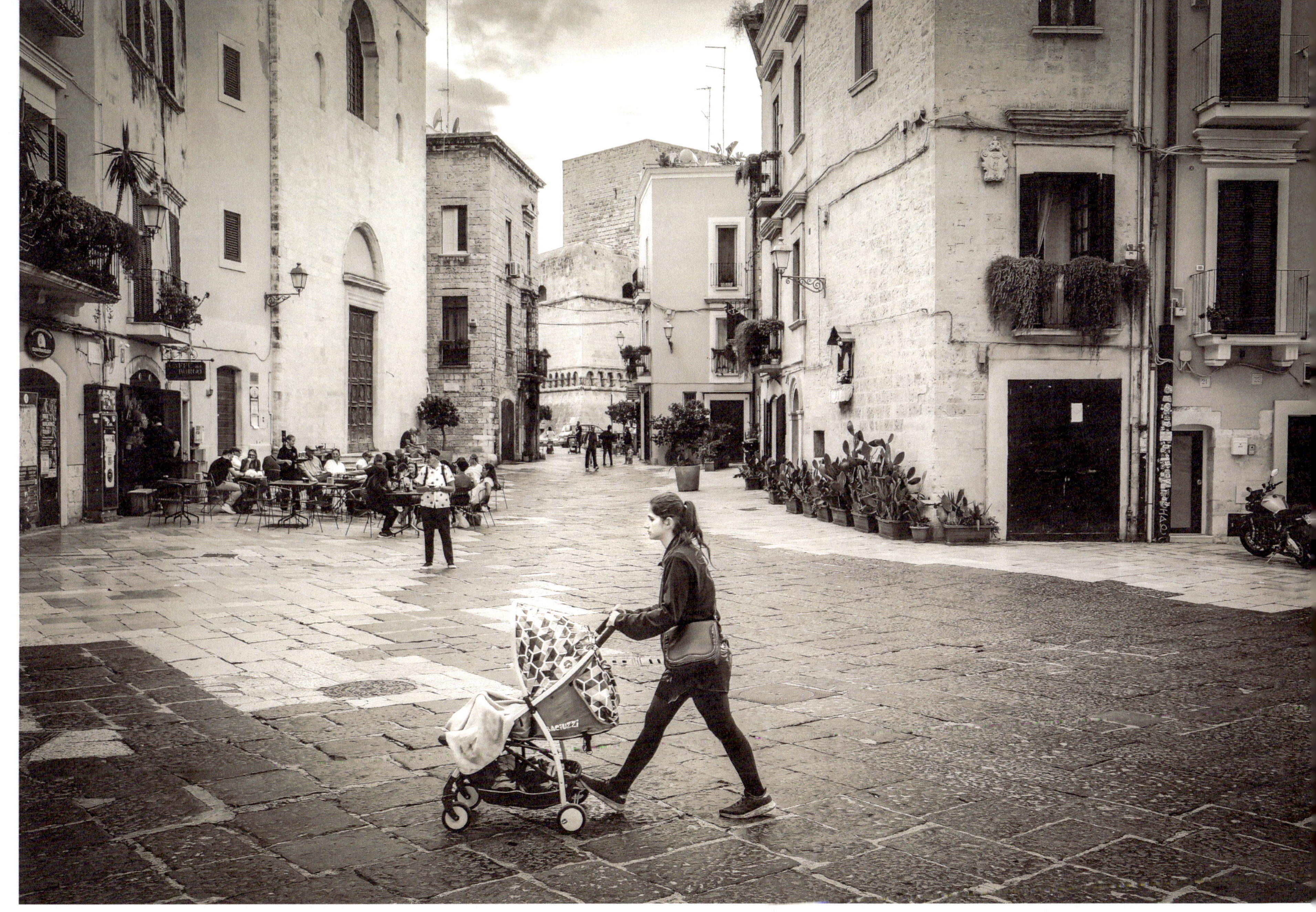

Baby Walker
Bari:
A girl strolls her nephew to sleep, dutifully babysitting for her working sister. Family dependence is a deeply rooted way of life in Italy.

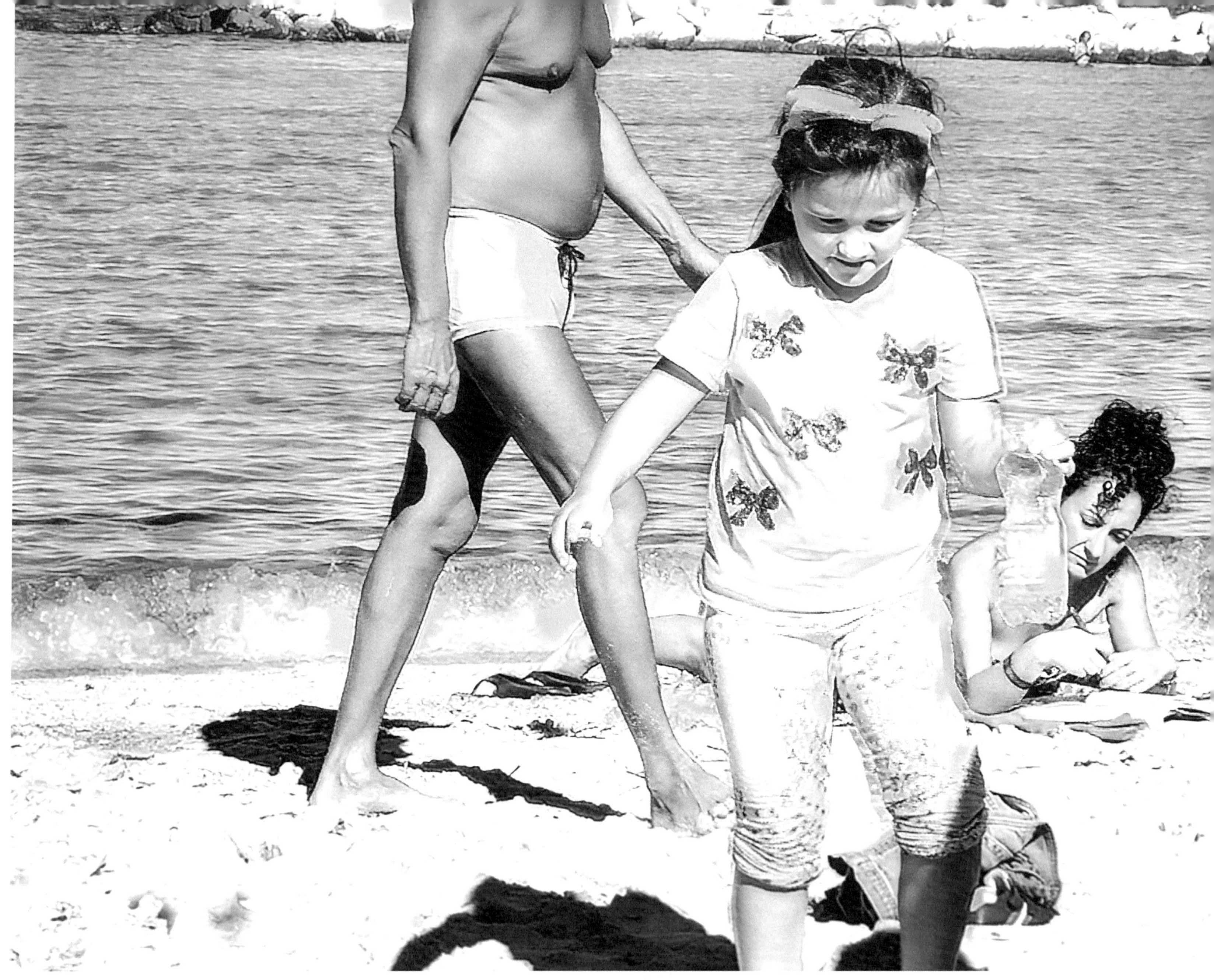

Beach Day
Bari:
A little girl fills a bottle of sea water to build a sand castle

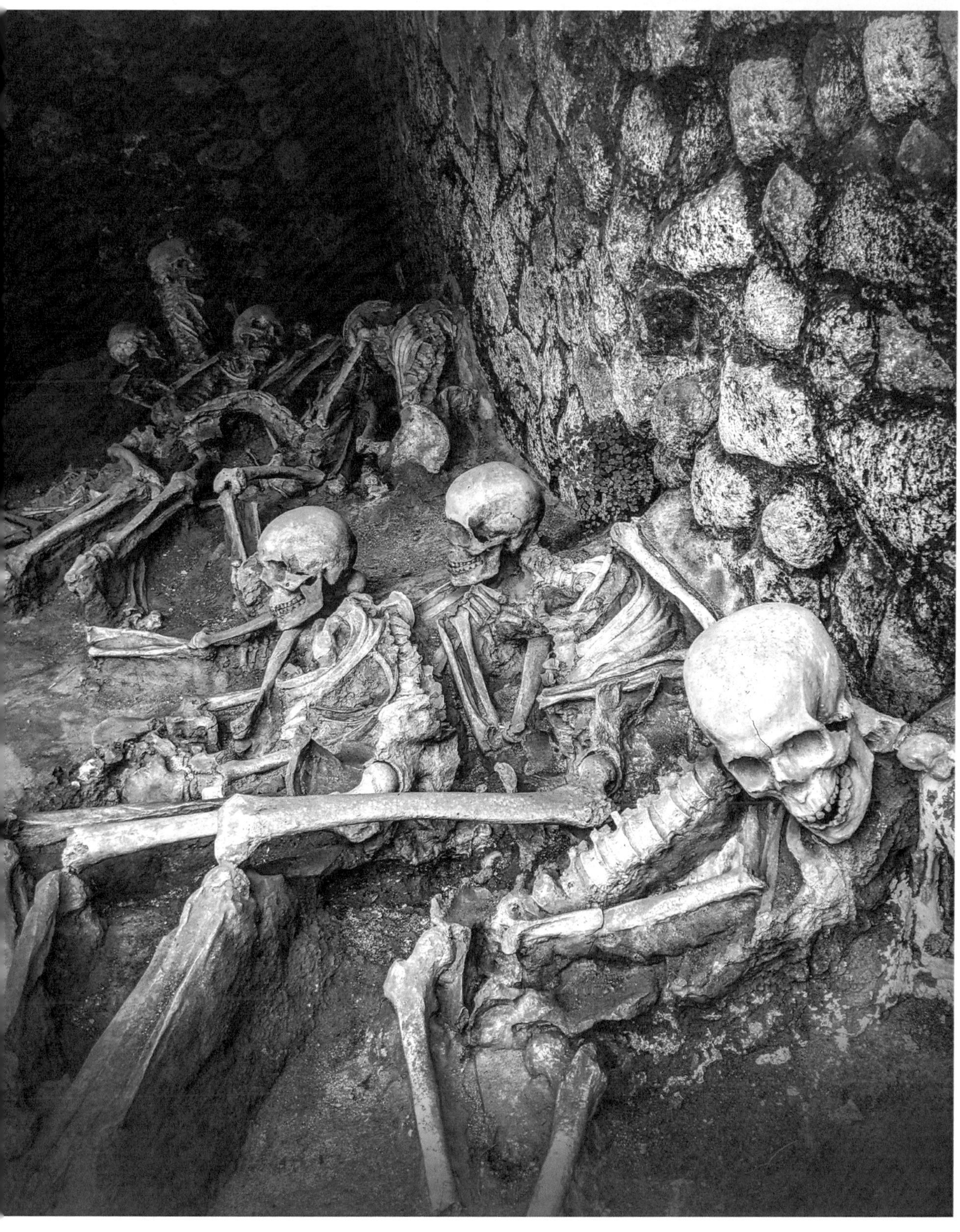

The Last Day

Herculaneum:
The sad vaporized remains of the terror filled victims of Vesuvius as it tore havock across the landscape 2000 years ago.

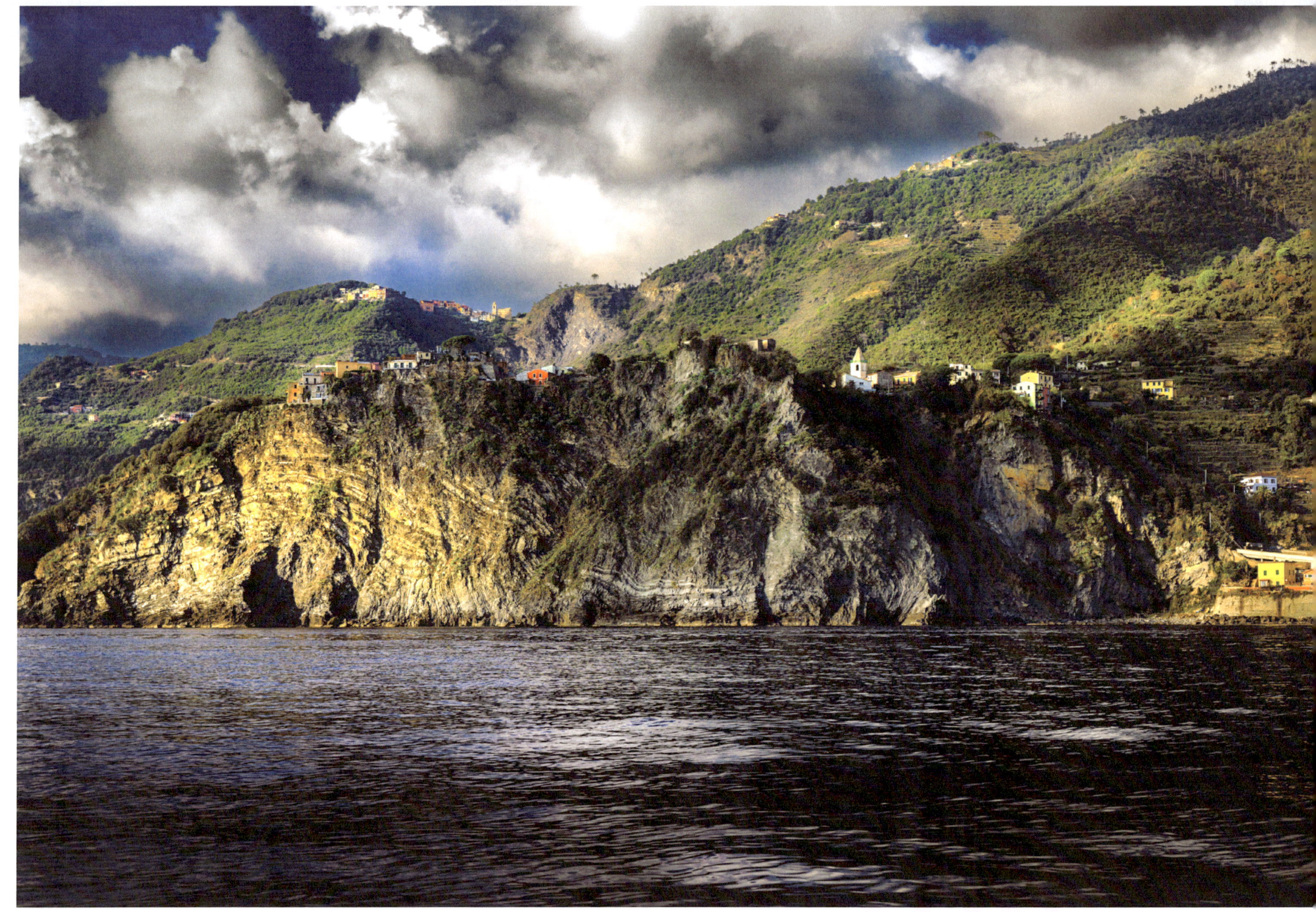

Aftermath Glow
Cinque Terre:
The tiny villages light up as the storm passes, casting an enchanting illumination at sunset in Cinque Terre.

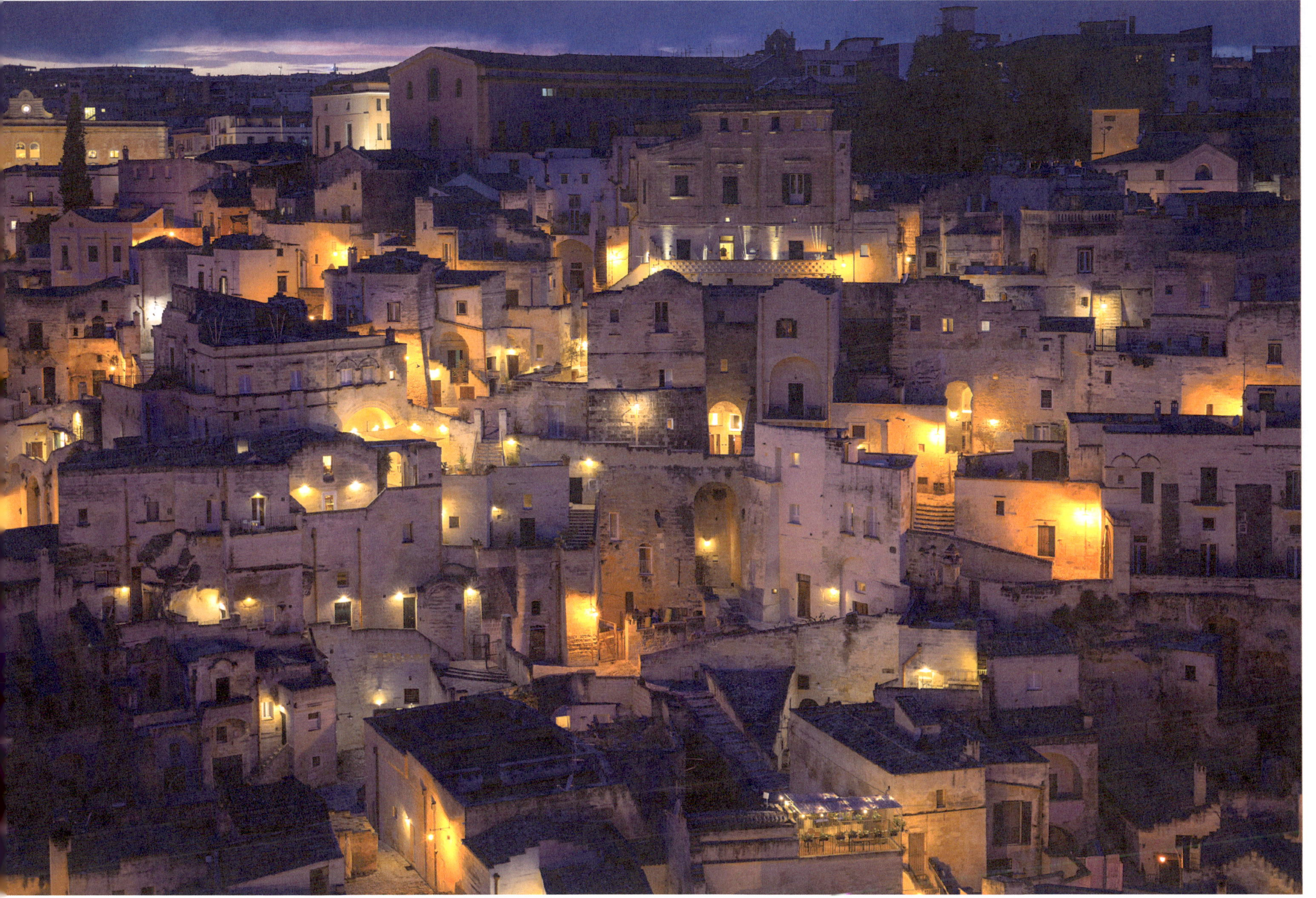

Enchanting Twilight
Matera:
As the sun sets, the ancient town of Matera begins to magically glow. In this town that has been continuosly
inhabited for 7000 years one can almost feel the presence of all the souls that have passed but still remain.

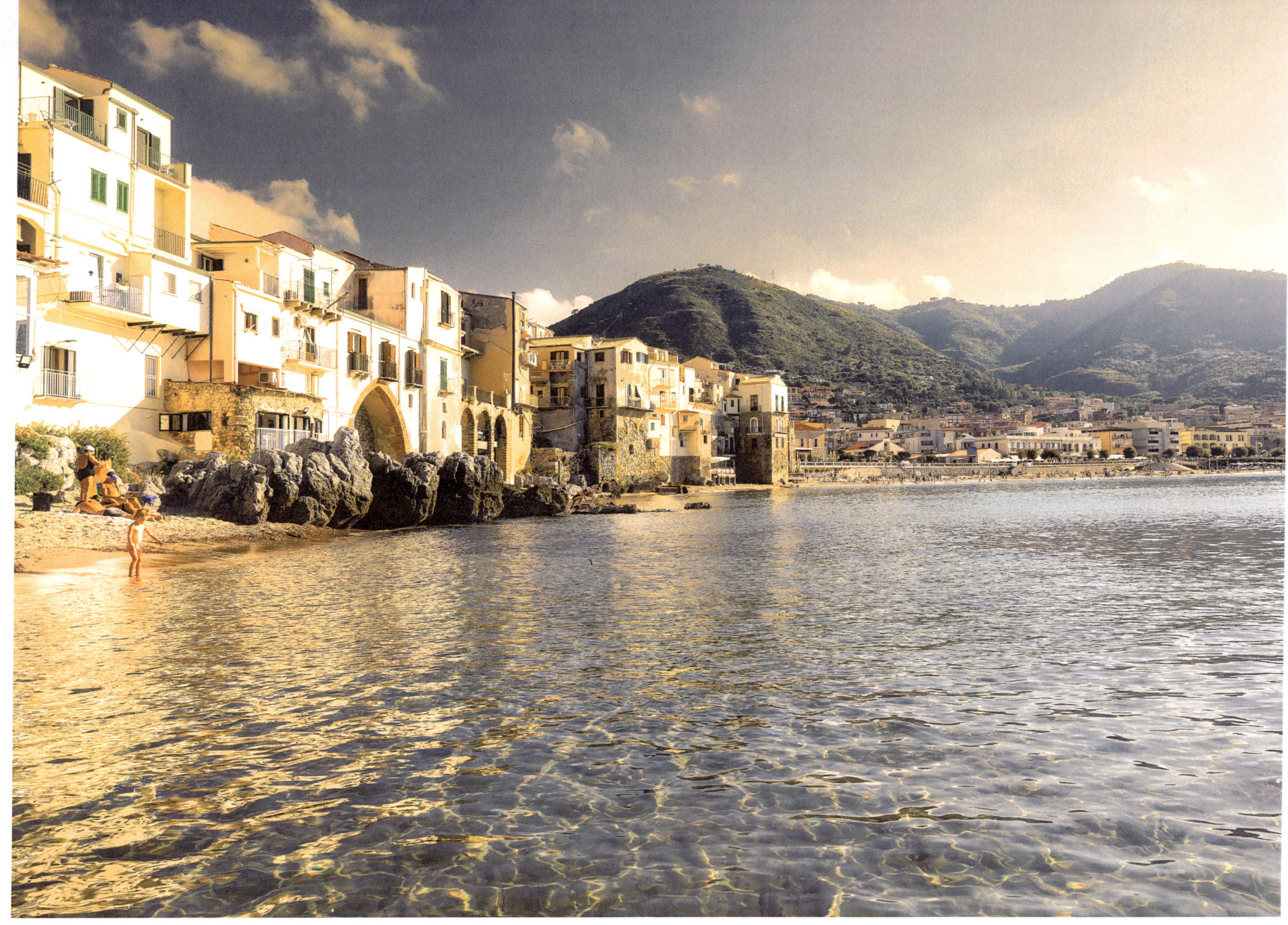

Stay a Little Longer
Cefalù:
A family soaks up the last rays of the sun as if time has stopped. A town so beautiful that I
have to close my eyes and open them to be sure it is real.

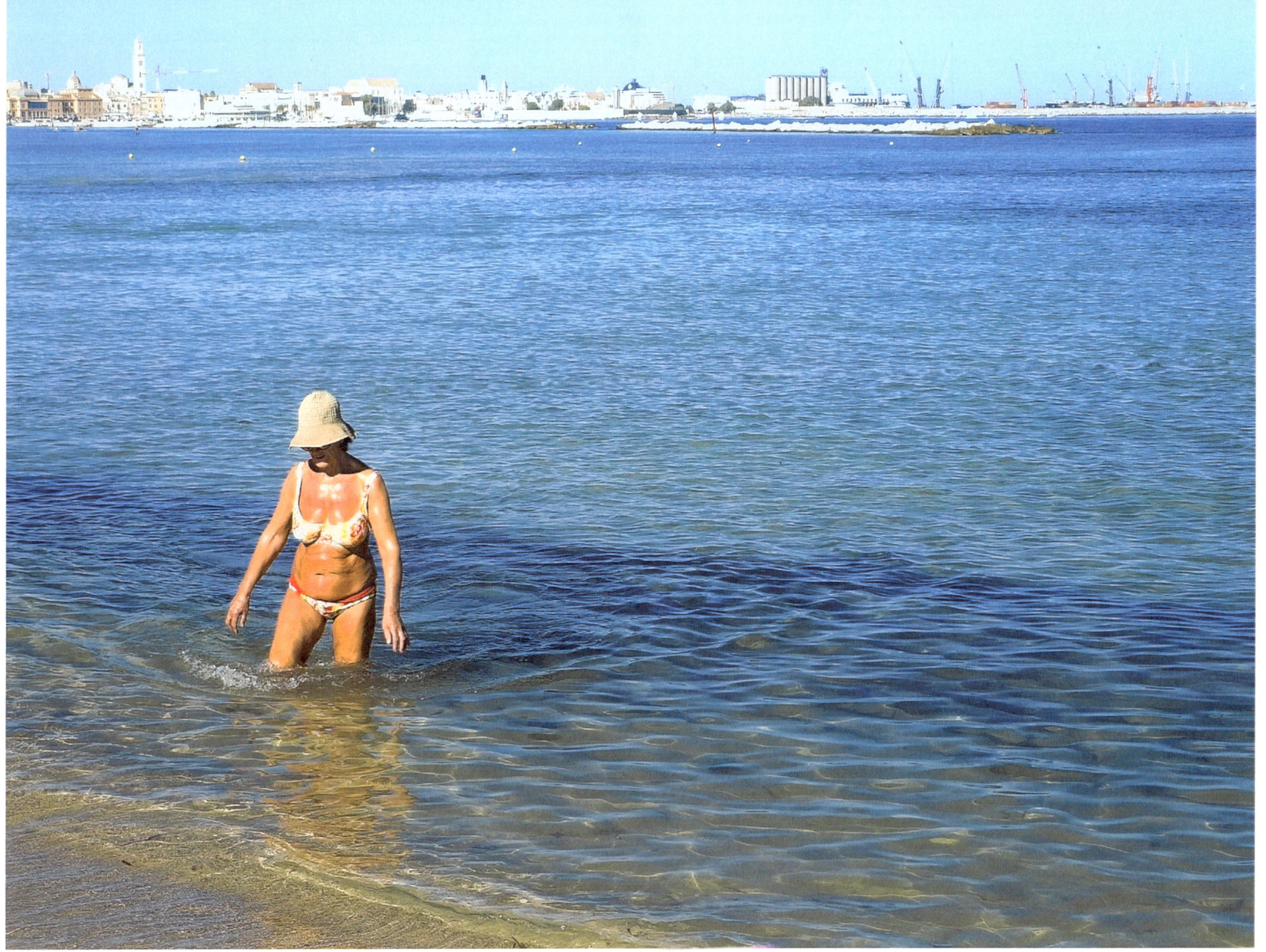

Morning Solitude
Bari:
Just after dawn, a woman enjoys a solitary swim in the calm waters of Bari.

The Fruit Man
Ortigia:
A hard working vendor endures another long, hot day selling oranges under the scorching midday sun. With so many vendors selling perishable goods the competition is quite challenging as expressed on the faces of these sidewalk business owners.

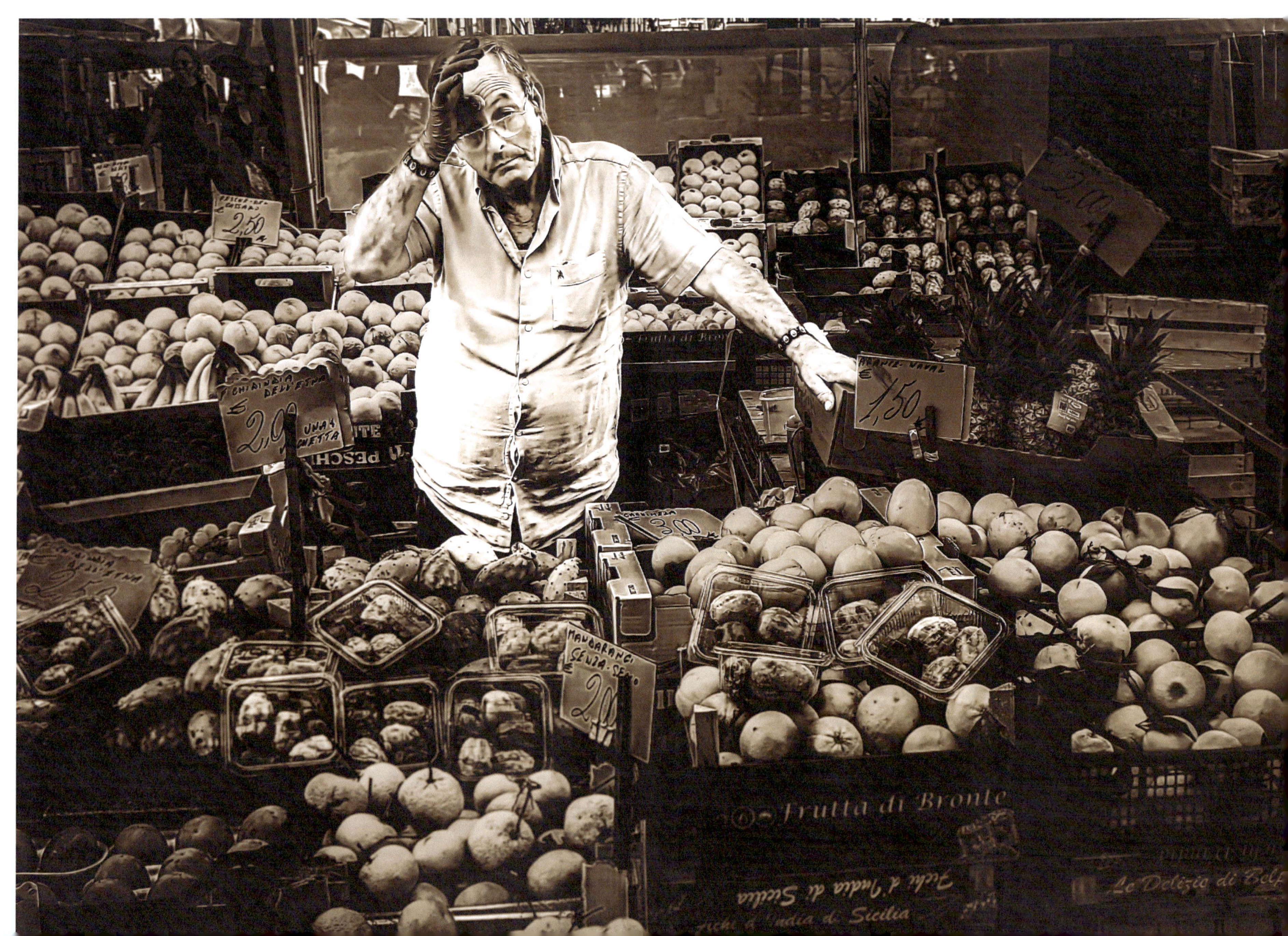

Canine Companions
Bari:
The palm lined pedestrian lane in Bari serves as a scenic evening walkway for this petsitter and his furry clients. Called the Corso Vittorio Emanuele, this lane divides the historic center from the modern city and leads it's wide eyed walkers to the majestic harbor.

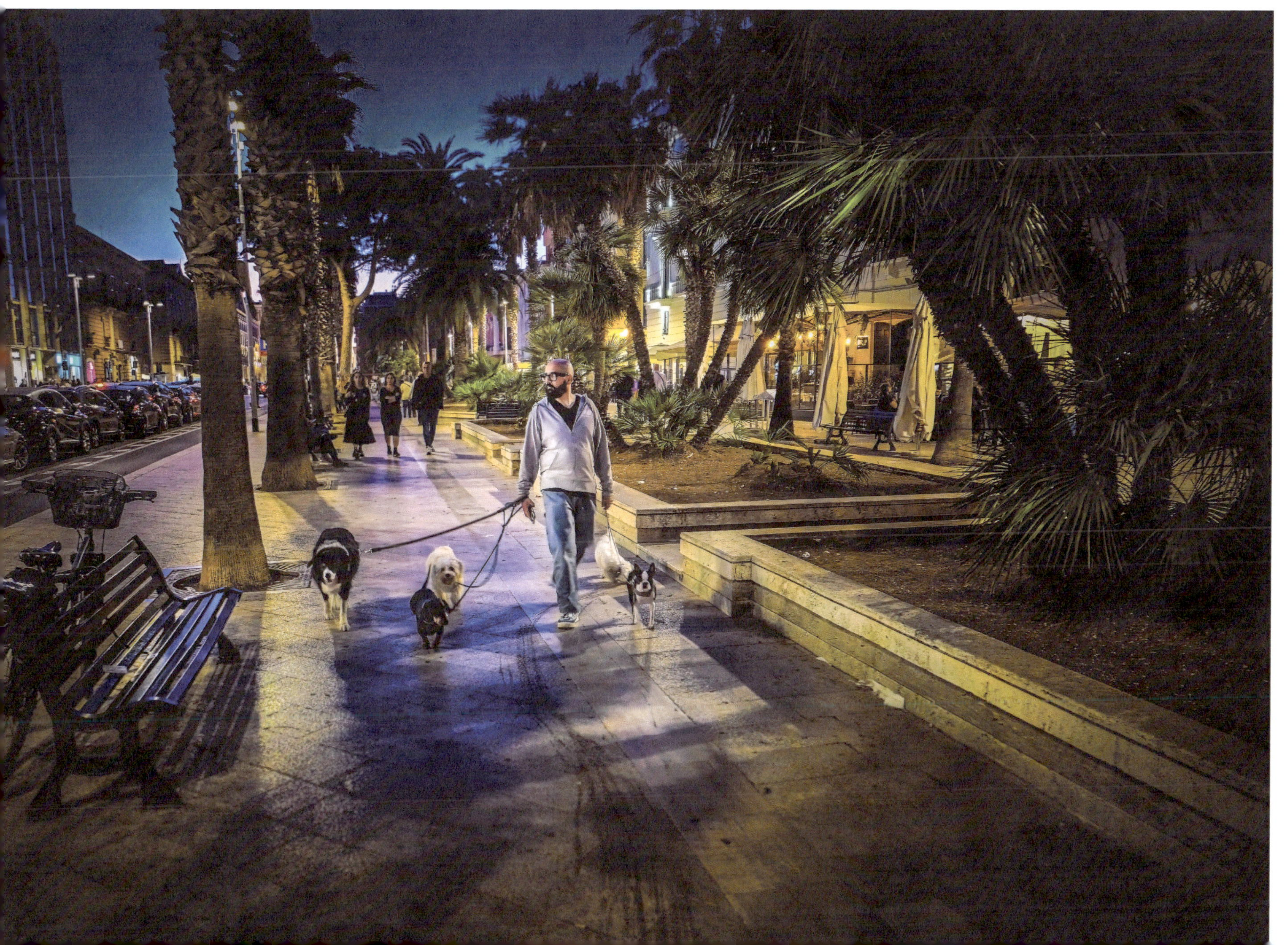

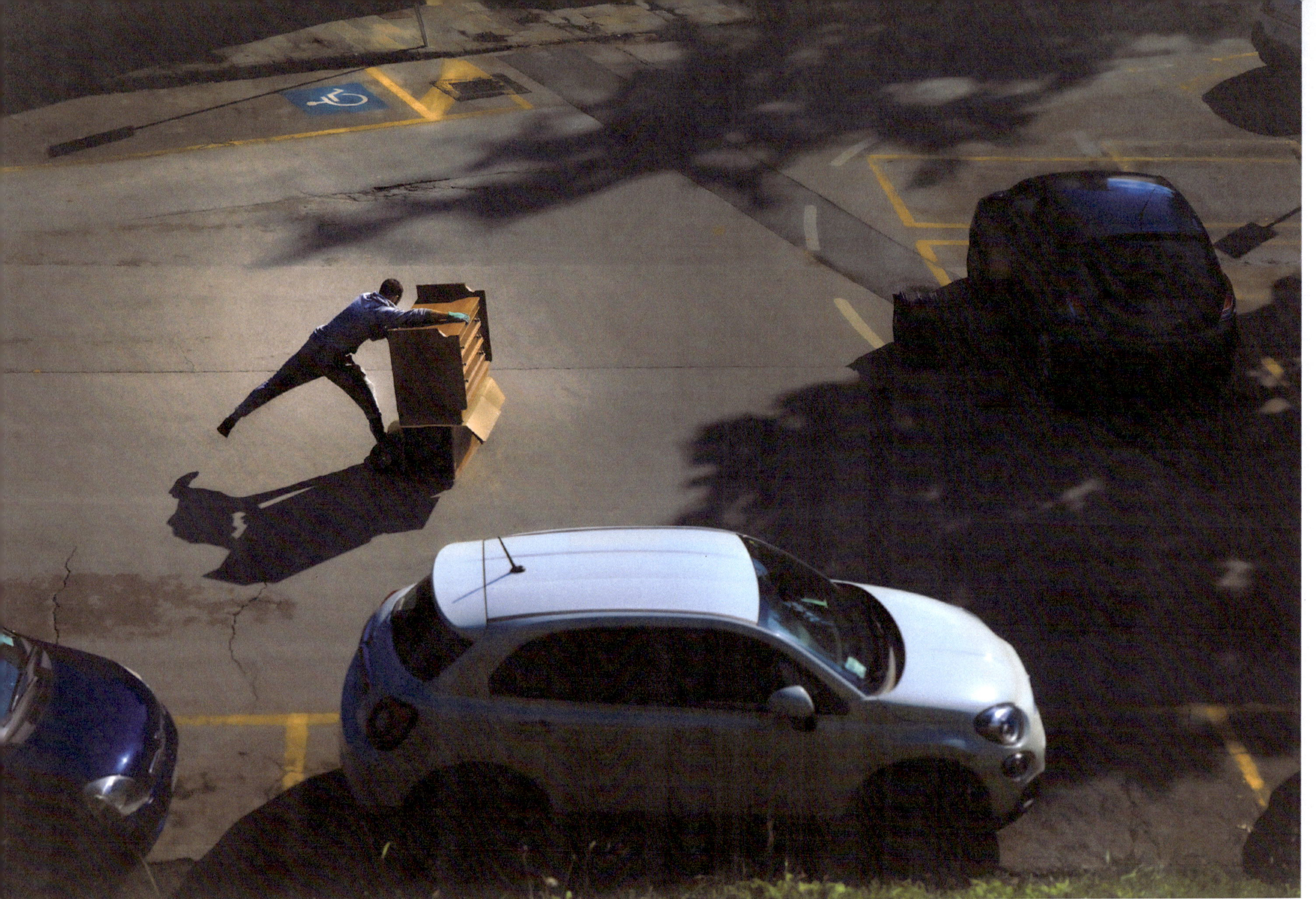

Moving Day
Lucca:
A man struggles to balance his dresser as he moves it across the street into a new apartment...without leaving a trace of a fingerprint.

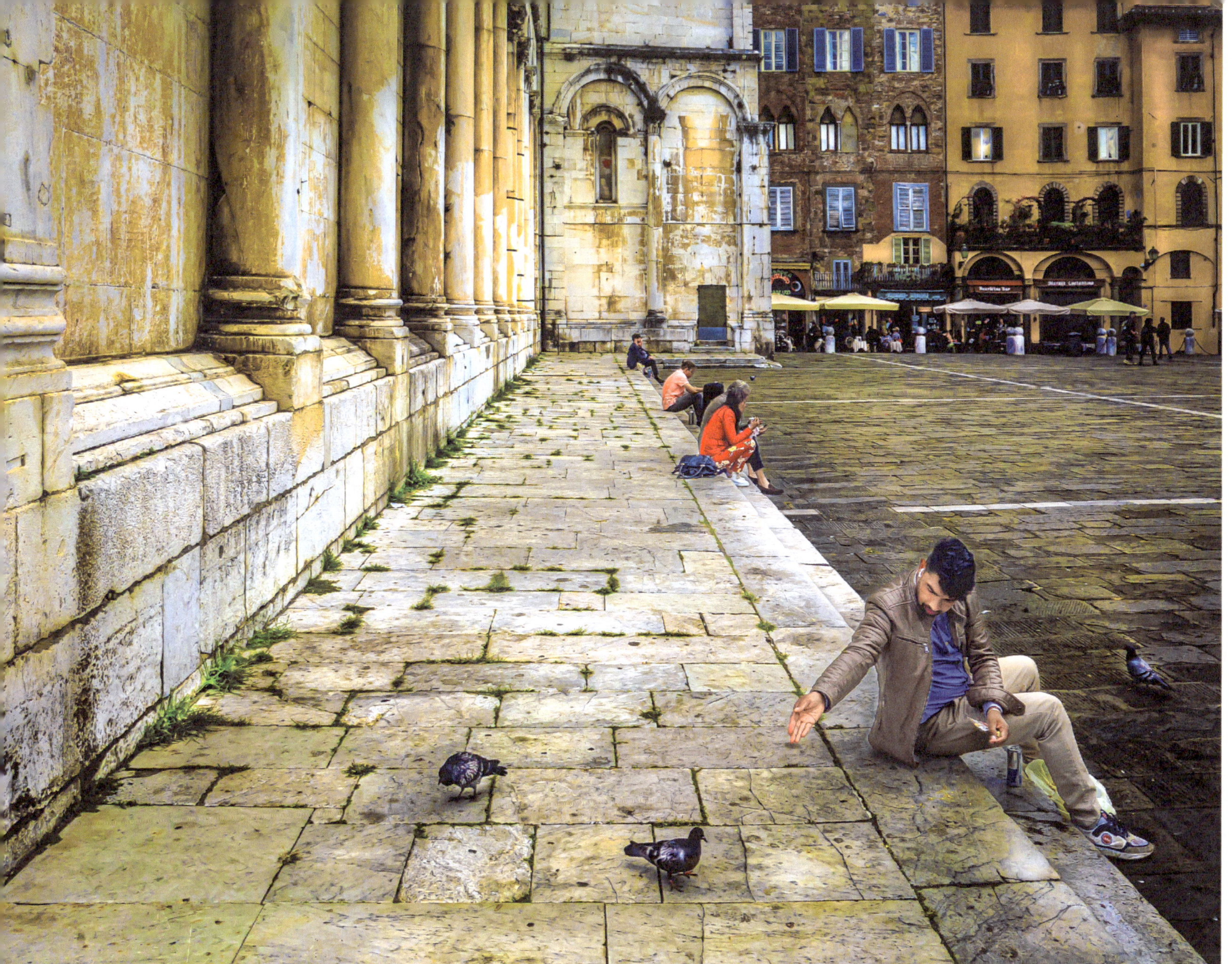

Birdman
Lucca:
A local offers his friendship and snacks to an interested but cautious pidgeon.

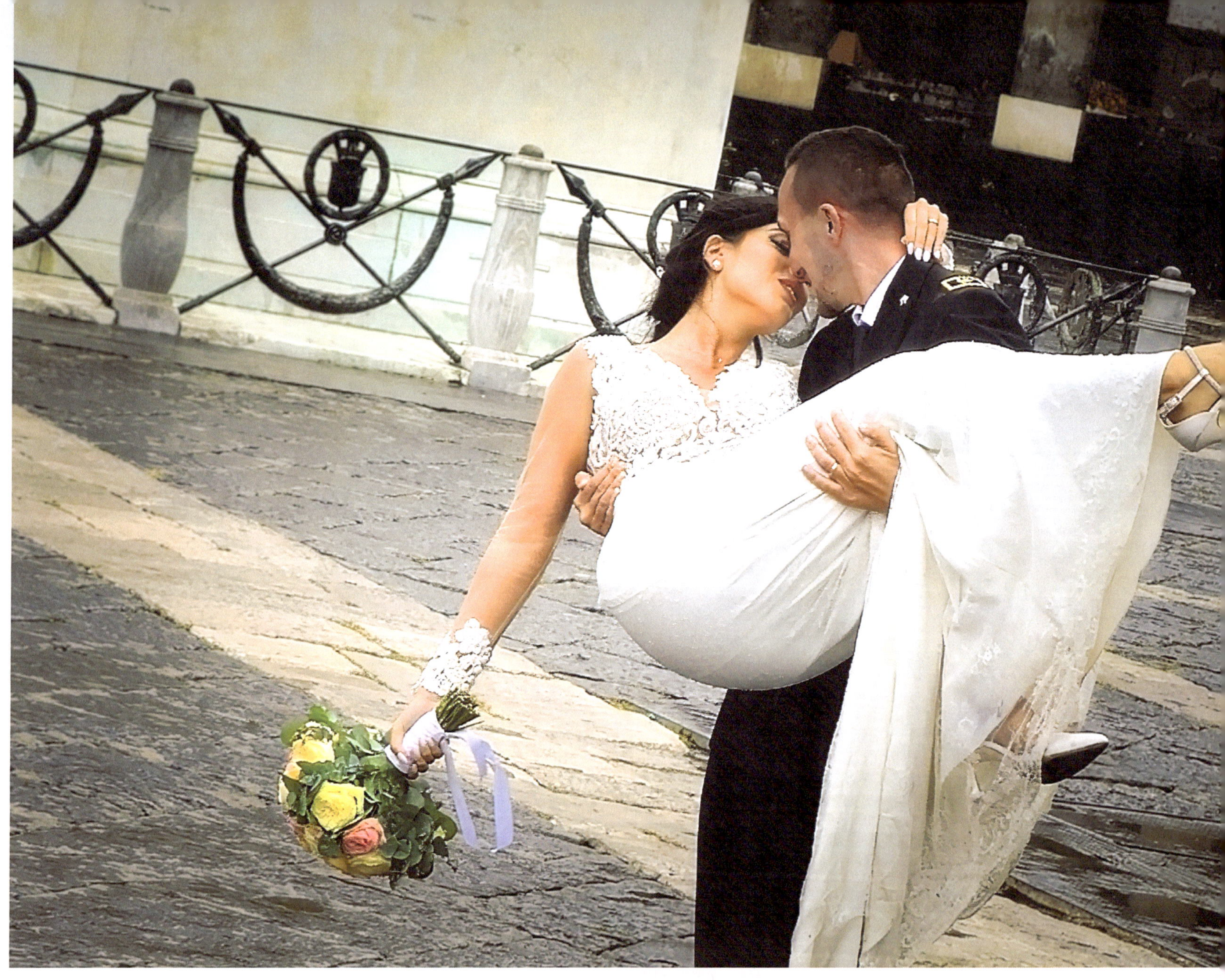

The Kiss
Naples
Newly weds share an emotional and picture perfect kiss outside the walls of the ancient cathedral

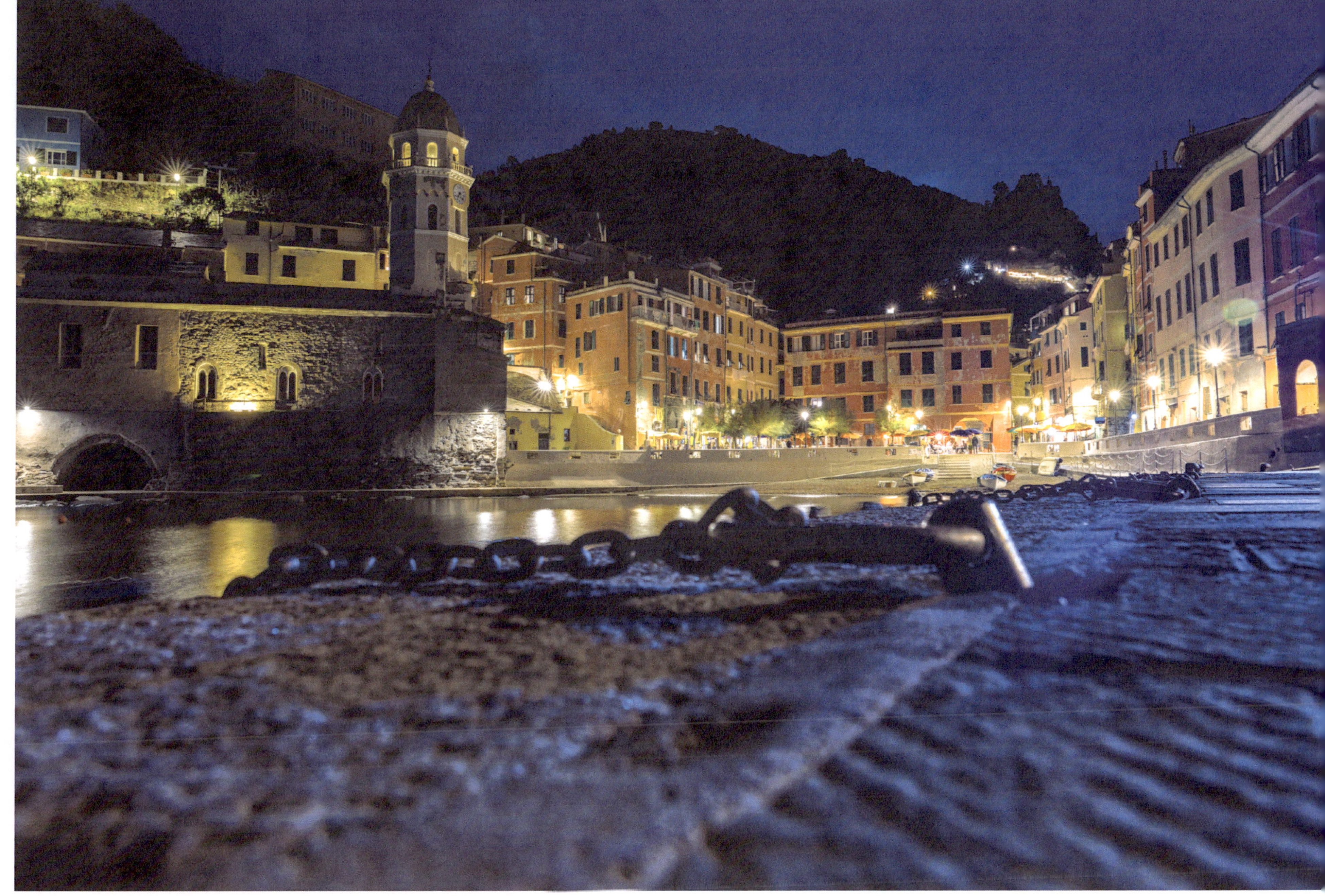

Nocturnal Palette
Vernazza:
The town takes on a candlelit appearance as daylight fades away revealing a
set from some romantic novel.

Ancient Dwellings
Matera:
Over 7000 years ago, humans first occupied the caves in this ravine, marking one of the oldest settlements in history. Standing in this spot at sunset is a hauntingly unique experience.

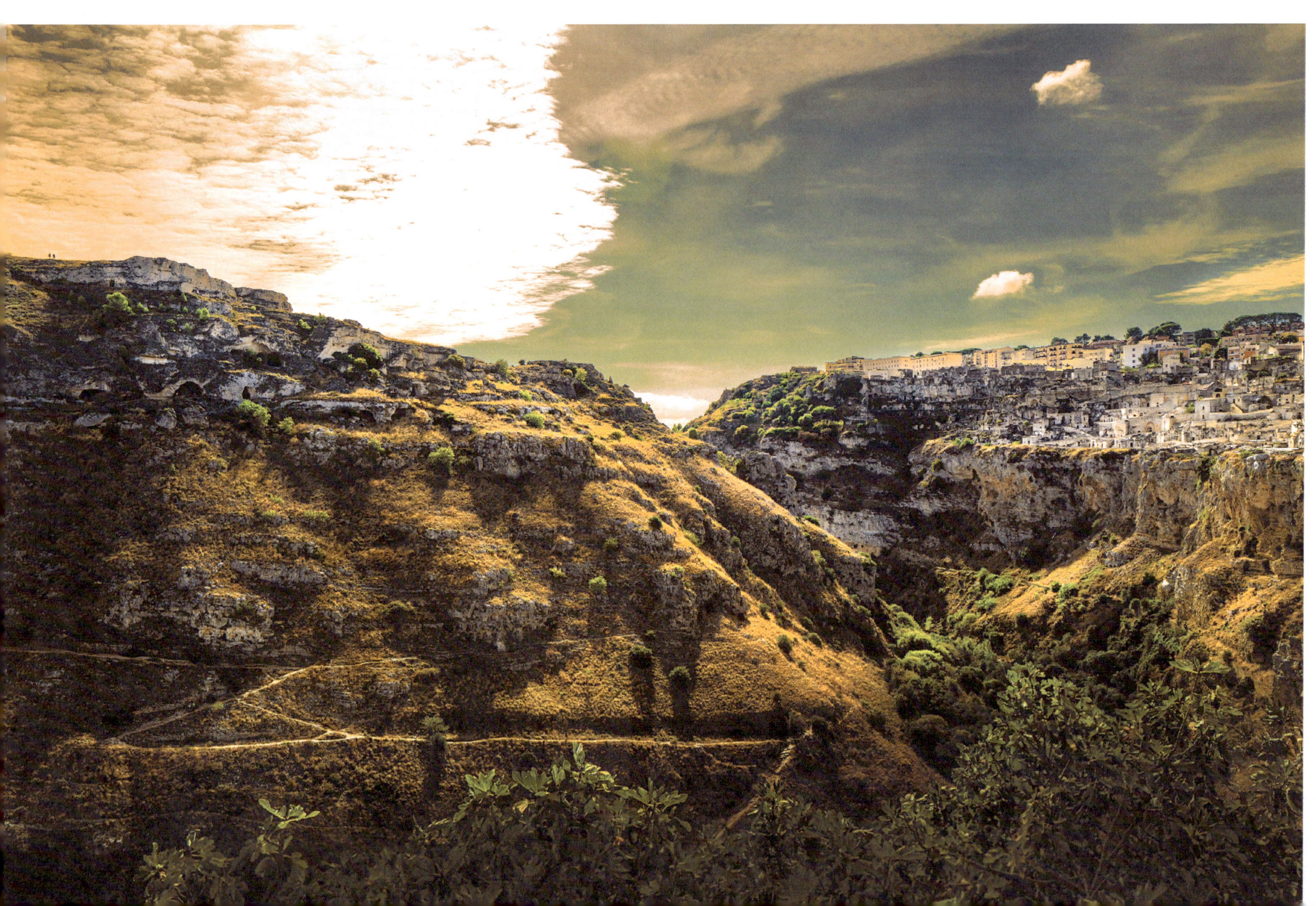

Sunset

Vernazza:
The hues of sunset washes the little town in a golden glow of visual riches. It is one of those spectacular scenes that one just marvels at until the darkness overtakes the heavenly light.

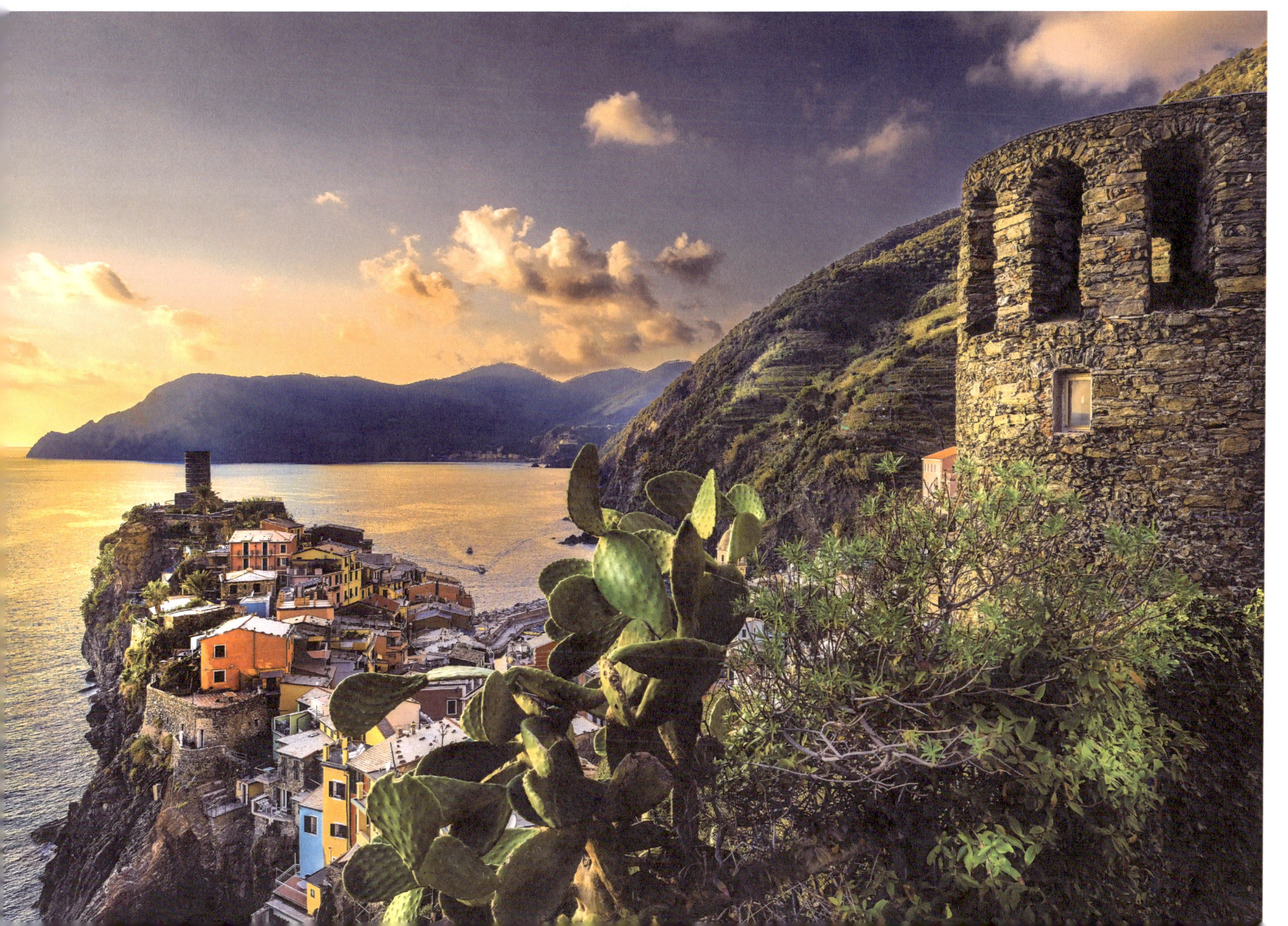

Boat workers walk home, a quiet procession marking the end of the day just as many have done for hundreds c
years past this ancient wall. New and old seamlessly blending together everywhere one looks

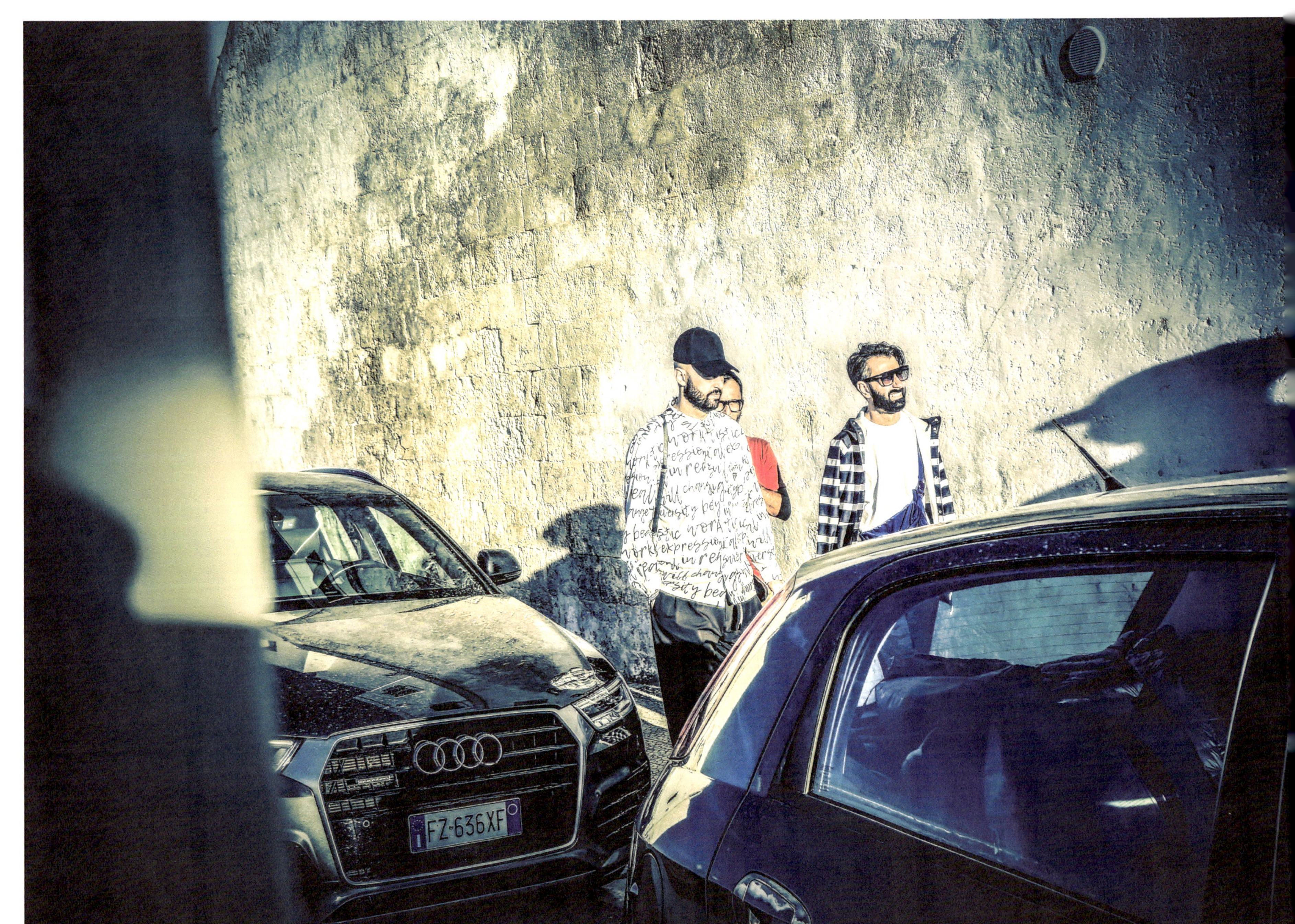

Aerial Thief
Ortigia:
A bold pidgeon seizes the moment of opportunity, like an aerial pickpocket,
catching these tourists off guard.

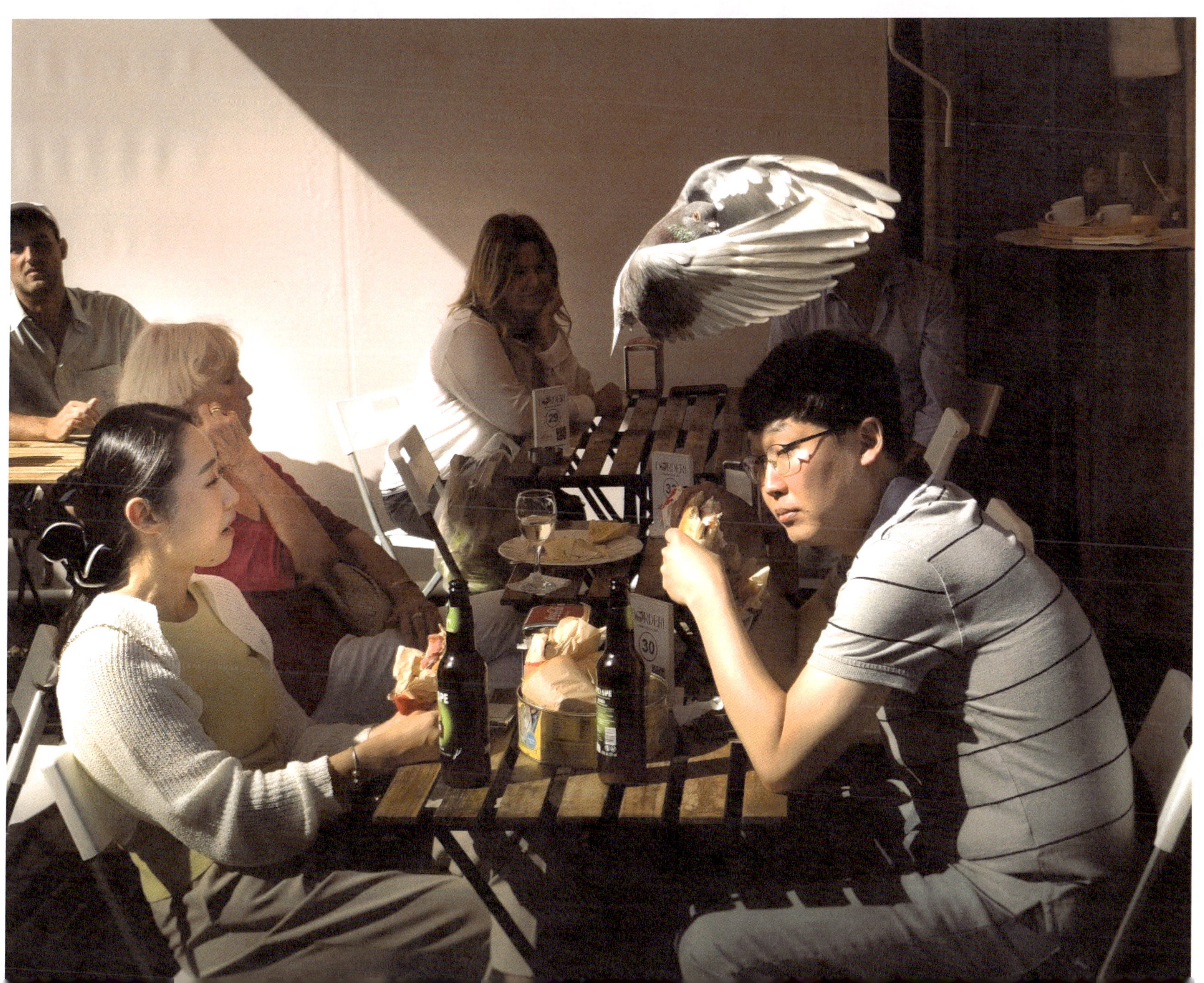

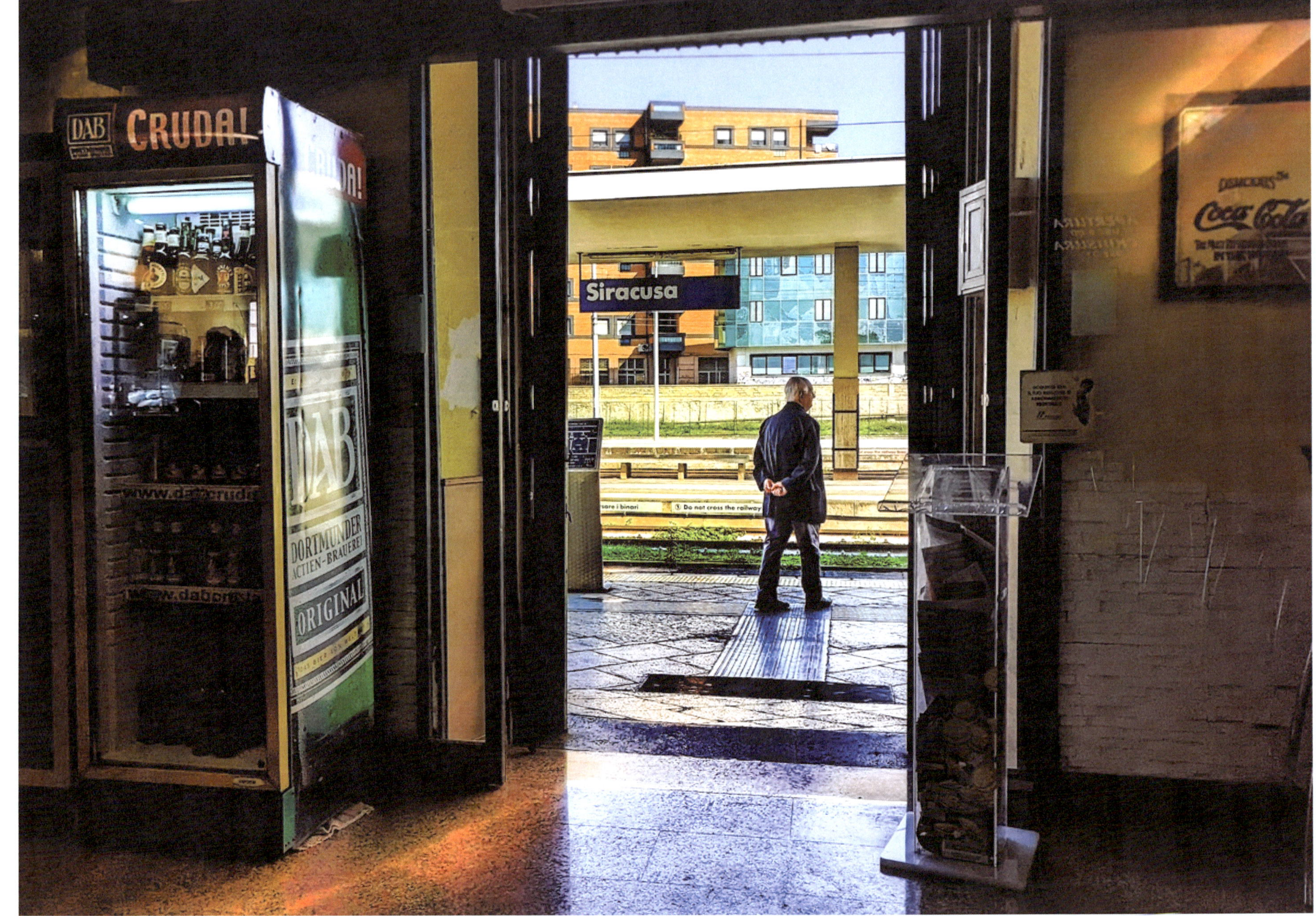

The Early Train
Siracusa:
A local gentleman keeps watch for his train and far away from my camera
in the coffee shop.

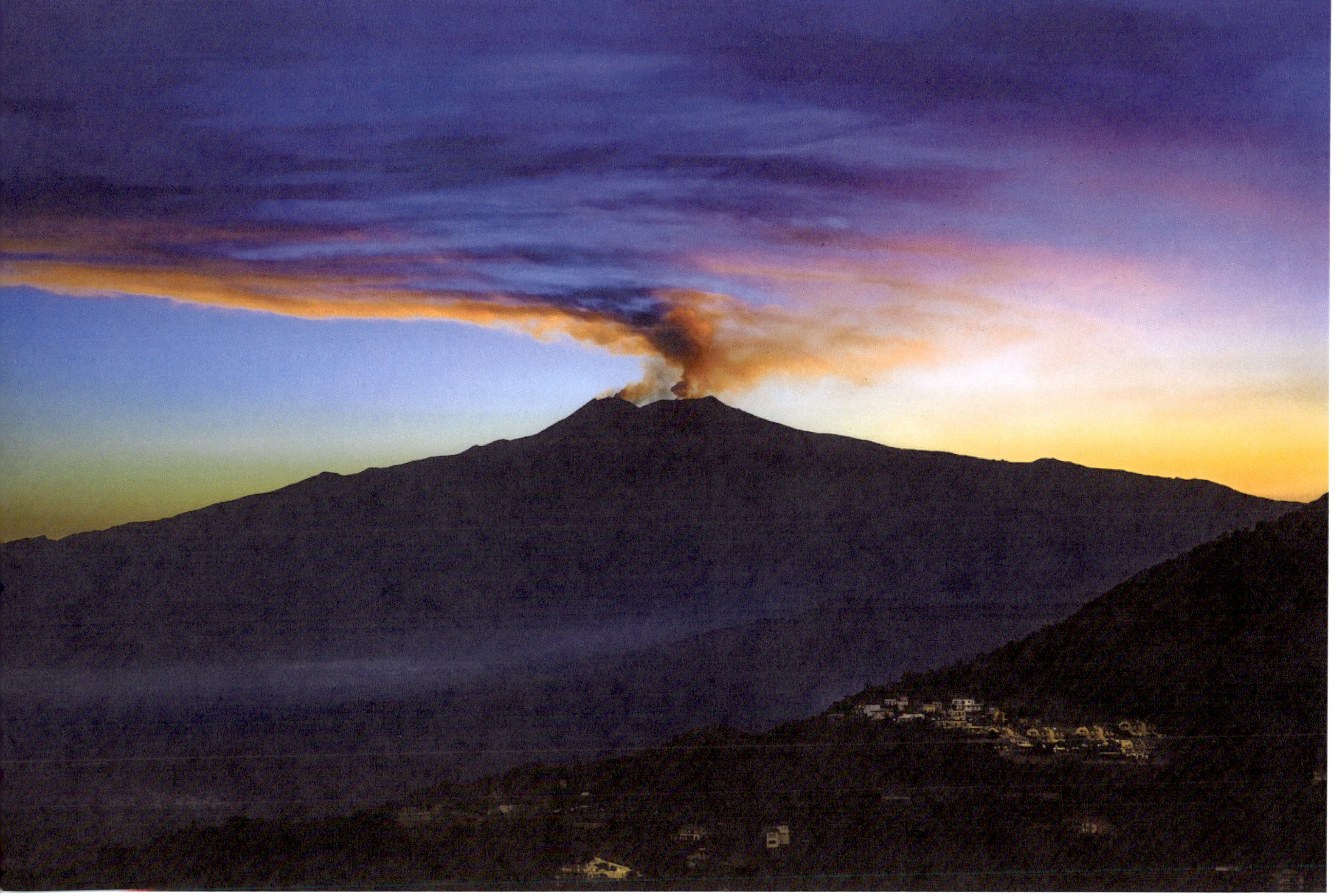

ETNA

Taormina:

This active volcano breathing in the morning sun as if warning all of its
power and might.